To Bill H[...]

May [...]

keep it in the short

grass!

Walter J. Austin, Jr.

JOHNNY GOODMAN
THE LAST AMATEUR GOLFER TO WIN
THE UNITED STATES OPEN
WITH
OBSERVATIONS ON
MEN'S AND WOMEN'S GOLF,
PAST AND PRESENT

by
Walter John Curtis, Sr., CLU

*Dedicated to preserving the history of a great
American amateur golfer - Johnny Goodman*

JOHNNY GOODMAN
The Last Amateur Golfer to Win
the United States Open

Library of Congress
Catalogue Card #96-96292

ISBN #0-9659419-0-6

Published by
W. J. Curtis, Sr.
P. O. Box 17693
Richmond, Virginia 23226

For ordering information,
please turn to the final page of the book.

FIFTEEN CENTS

June 6, 1938

TIME

The Weekly Newsmagazine

Color photograph for TIME by Paul Dorsey

Volume XXXI

GOLFER JOHNNY GOODMAN
The king of swing?
(See SPORT)

Number 23

iii

About the Author

The author of this book, Walter J. Curtis, Sr., was introduced to championship golf at age 12 as a caddie at The Country Club in Brookline, Massachusetts. This is one of the nation's oldest and finest courses, steeped in golf history, and the venue for many National Championships.

He has been an avid golfer all of his life, and has traveled widely as an astute observer of championship golf in the United States and the British Isles.

He served as an officer in the 5th Fighter Command of the United States Air Force in the South Pacific during World War II. He retired as Vice President and Chief Agency and Marketing Officer after 40 years with Home Beneficial Life, a leading life insurance company in Richmond, Virginia.

He presently is a public relations representative in preventive medicine for the Virginia Heart Institute in Richmond, Virginia.

His keen observation and interest in golf, and especially championship golf, has spanned his lifetime. His great enthusiasm for golf has motivated him to write this compelling biography of Johnny Goodman, and to share his views on the evolution of the game over the last half century.

DEDICATION

This book is especially dedicated to the wife of Johnny Goodman, Josephine, and to the many fine people of Nebraska who gave Johnny a helping hand along the way.

CONTENTS

PART I: THE LIFE AND CAREER
OF JOHNNY GOODMAN
CHAPTER I
The Early Years .... ,,,,.............................. 27

CHAPTER II
Gaining Prominence In The Golf
World At Pebble Beach, California 43

CHAPTER III
Johnny Goodman's Play In The Years
Immediately Following Pebble Beach 61

CHAPTER IV
Winning The Premier Event: The 1933
United States Open Golf Tournament...................... 67

LIST OF ILLUSTRATIONS

FOREWORD

Those golfers who are aficionados and devoted fans of golf and its history will find this book, with its humor, fun to read. It will greatly add to their knowledge of the great game of golf over the last half century to the present. I think they will find the life story of Johnny Goodman, the last amateur to win the United States Open, to be fascinating.

The history of the game of golf, past and present, is rich in drama and excitement, and this book surely adds to the store of that history.

Marvin (Vinny) Giles, III
Former United States and
British Amateur Champion

ACKNOWLEDGMENTS

I would like to acknowledge my gratitude for the sources of information for this biography of Johnny Goodman: Johnny Goodman's widow, Josephine Goodman, and his only son, John; his nephew in Omaha, Jack Atkins; The Historical Society of Omaha, Nebraska; *The World Herald* newspaper of Omaha; The Omaha Field Club's historical records; The Nebraska Golf Hall of Fame; The Historical Society of Douglas County, Nebraska; The USGA's Library at its headquarters in Far Hills, New Jersey; The Historical Records at The Augusta National Golf Course, Augusta, Georgia; excerpts from the writings of Charles Bartlett, of *The Chicago Tribune*; Robert T. Jones, Jr.; William D. Richardson, of *The New York Times*; Grantland Rice, and John F. Gleason, golf historian of Florida. Also, members of the 1938 Walker Cup Team: Charles Kocis, Charles Yeats, Fred Haas, Jr., and Willie Turnesa. For permission to use excerpts from the book *The Golf Hall of Shame*, by Bruce Nash and Allen Zullo; and Tim Rosaforte, curator, Pocket Books of Simon & Schuster, Inc.; *Time, Inc.*, for permission granted to use the June 6, 1938 cover.

I'm grateful for the helpful comments on the manuscript from Robert Wrenn, one of Richmond's professional golf favorites and outstanding member of the PGA tour. He was winner of the 1987 Buick Open with a 72 hole total of 262 (26 under par), within one stroke of the all time PGA Tour 72 hole scoring record held by Ben Hogan and Mike Souchak. I'm also grateful for the insightful suggestions and comments made by Richmond's own amateur golf star, Marvin (Vinny) Giles, past United States and British Amateur Champion.

Credit also needs to be given to my wife, Marta, a former English teacher, who reviewed these writings and kept grammatical errors to a minimum; to my son, W. John Curtis, and to T. R. Hollingsworth, who both did some effective editing, and to my secretary, Jean Hudson; without their efforts this book wouldn't have reached fruition.

RATIONALE

I have three reasons for writing this book: to preserve the history of one of America's great amateur golfers; to reveal a fascinating story of the rise of a golfer to stardom from an humble beginning, overcoming almost insurmountable obstacles on the way; and to document a life story in order to provide inspiration for those who could follow in his footsteps.

QUOTES

This story is written through the eyes of an amateur, and here are some quotes that I think all amateurs can identify with. The three quotes below were taken from the USGA Golf House Exhibit, Far Hills, New Jersey.

"Golf was first a game for rough-hewn Scots trying to figure a way to get someone else to pay for their drinks. Then it became an outdoor pastime for the gentry. Now it has become inexorably woven in the fabric of popular sports. Like the yips, once it gets you, it never lets go."

Peter Andrews

"It is reasonable to assume that in the last five years Americans have collectively lost more than one billion golf balls, and yet, golfers keep coming back for more. Surely, no other sporting endeavor can match that kind of dogged perseverance in the face of such manifest futility."

Peter Andrews

"In the end, all golfers are after the same thing - those sweet and elusive moments when all the pieces finally come together and they find themselves playing that cool, quiet golf, that game within the game we all know exists, the one we know we can get to if we can just stop wanting it long enough to let it happen."

David Noonan

Those who enjoy sports of all varieties can easily identify with the following quote:

"I always turn to the sports page first. The sports page records people's accomplishments; the front page nothing but man's failures."

Earl Warren, former Chief
Justice of the United States
Supreme Court (1891 - 1974)

Some quotes of my own:

"A true golfer is endlessly adjusting his swing. Like a woman and her weight-she is either losing it, gaining it, or redistributing it."

Walter Curtis

"Every avid golfer has some Don Quixote ideas of competing endlessly to conquer the game of golf. This is one of the reasons this game can be so addictive."

Walter Curtis

Johnny Goodman's
Tournament Golf Record

Johnny Goodman's record of achievements in golf goes well beyond the last amateur to win the United States Open golf tournament. Some of them are as follows:

- Won 60 golf tournaments in his career, the first being the Omaha, Nebraska City Championship at the age of 16.
- Won the Trans-Mississippi Tournament at the age of 18 in 1927, and again in 1931 and 1935.
- Won the Nebraska State Amateur in 1929.
- Won the Mexican Amateur in 1936 and 1937.
- Came into national prominence for the first time by defeating Bobby Jones in the first round of the National Amateur in 1929 at the famed Pebble Beach Golf Course in California. At the time, Bobby Jones was considered the greatest golfer in the world.
- Finalist in the 1932 National Amateur, losing two and one, but not before upsetting Francis Ouimet, former winner of the U. S. Open, in the semifinals
- Low amateur in the United States Open in 1932.
- Won the United States Open in 1933 by setting a course record in the second round of 66. He was the fourth golfer up to that time to ever break par in the United States Open for four rounds. Johnny, at this writing, was the last amateur to win the United States Open.
- Finalist in the 1934 National Amateur.
- Low amateur in the 1935 United States Open.
- Won the 1937 National Amateur.
- Low amateur and tied for eighth in the 1937 United States Open.
- Played on three consecutive Walker Cup Teams representing the United States in 1934, 1936, and 1938.

THE ELITE
WINNERS OF THE U.S. AMATEUR
AND
THE U.S. OPEN

NAME	AMATEUR	OPEN
Jerome De Travers	1907-08-12-13	1915
Francis Ouimet	1914-31	1913
Chick Evans	1916-20	1916
Robert T. Jones, Jr.	1924-25-27-28-30	1923-26-29-30
Lawson Little	1934-35	1940
Johnny Goodman	1937	1933
Gene Littler	1953	1961
Arnold Palmer	1954	1960
Jack Nicklaus	1959-61	1962-67-72-80
Jerry Pate	1974	1976

INTRODUCTION

So that you may know where I am coming from, I was a young lad of 12 growing up in the depths of America's Great Depression when I was introduced to championship golf, caddieing at The Country Club in Brookline, Massachusetts. In 1932 I had a chance to watch the Walker Cup matches being played there. This was the seventh series of matches between the best United States amateurs playing against the best of Britain. The British had lost in the previous six years, and lost again that year. I was impressed with a member of the British team, Cyril Tolley, two-time British Amateur Champion. When he teed off, he never used a wooden tee - he simply drove from where he tossed the ball on the turf. For some reason, that memory stuck in my mind.

As an interesting sidelight, that year Briton Leonard Crawley, a member of the British team, hooked an iron shot to the spot where the big silver cup was on display, and knocked it off its pedestal. It has been said that was the nearest the British ever came to putting a dent in the Walker Cup. As they say, though, time changes nearly everything, for in 1995 the British defeated the Americans in the Walker Cup matches held in Great Britain. However, the American team has not held a total lock on the Walker Cup, as the British also won in 1938, 1971, and 1989.

It was September, 1934. The National Amateur was being played at The Country Club in Brookline on a course founded in 1895. This club was one of the original four members of the United States Golf Association. The course is steeped in golf history, being the same course on which the famous golfer, Francis Ouimet, caddied - the same course on which he won The United States Open in 1913 as an amateur, defeating the great English golfers Vardon and Ray. This was an event that turned the golf world on its ear. Ouimet was the first American born to win the Open and it was this fact more than any other that served to touch off the growth in popularity of golf in America. The Country Club[1] over the years has been the venue for many national golf events. It's a course that calls for the use of every club in the bag.

It was there that I first saw Johnny Goodman. He was not a tall man, about five feet, nine inches, blonde hair, handsome features, and rather slender - not someone who would invite special attention. My older brother, Vincent, caddied for Johnny Goodman in the National Amateur that year, 1934. He told me that Johnny was friendly and talkative. He thought, too, that he was a heck of a good golfer. What impressed me most was that my brother said he was a very liberal tipper; Johnny being a former caddy himself, I'm sure that experience had something to do with his generosity. Disappointingly, the fellow I caddied for, who was from California, lost his match in the first round, but this gave me a chance to watch the tournament throughout.

At that age I was more impressed by the golf professional at The Country Club than with anyone else. His strong British accent, elegant manner, and impeccable attire left a lasting impression on me. To my young mind, that's who I wanted to be like when I grew up.

This was the year that Lawson Little, son of an army colonel, won the Amateur and went on to win the Amateur and the British Amateur back to back in 1934 and 1935, quite a feat in itself. I don't recall being particularly impressed by the event, except that my mouth fell open and my eyes got

[1] *The Bi-annual Ryder Cup will be played at The Country Club in 1999, when the defeated Americans will attempt to regain the Cup from the Europeans; another example of its great venue for major tournaments.*

real wide when I saw Lawson Little drive the green on the all uphill 312-yard par four sixth hole during the championship.

The peak of my golf career was when I won a caddie tournament. The caddies were allowed to play the course at The Country Club on Mondays. That was a treat indeed. In winning the caddie tournament, I received a certificate to get a new pair of trousers, and, needless to say, I was just thrilled, especially since this was the first pair of new trousers I had ever received in my life. Being the youngest of a family of 13 children, I had a plentiful supply of hand-me-down clothes and very little money for anything new. These were the days when if you saw a penny on the sidewalk you were happy with your find and immediately picked it up. Today, many people wouldn't bother to pick up a penny on the ground, and would treat it as just another bit of litter. Needless to say, for those who remember it, the Depression colored the way you looked at life.

Later in life, I think I have subconsciously identified with Johnny Goodman, who also was from a poor family of 13 children. There the similarity ended.

PART I

The Life and Career of Johnny Goodman

CHAPTER I

The Early Years

The biography that is to unfold is truly an old-fashioned Horatio Alger success story. The unlikely life of John George Goodman began in an environment of poverty and disadvantage, hardly the background to enhance the development of a world-class golfer. His home was in the packing house district of Omaha, Nebraska, not one of the better residential areas. His mother and father, William and Rose, emigrated from Lithuania to the state of Pennsylvania at about the turn of the 20th Century, but then headed west to Omaha. Their fifth child was Johnny, born December 28, 1908, at 4128 South 36th Street.

Johnny first appeared in the news in 1916, when, at the age of seven, he got diphtheria. Omaha health officers, upon going to the Goodman home, found Johnny sleeping with three other children in one bed, and four more Goodman children in another bed in the same room. Mother Goodman, accustomed to peasant ways, refused to send Johnny to an isolation hospital or keep him from the other children. The health authorities, unable to find a law to compel Mother Goodman to do what she did not want to do with her brood, slapped a black sign marked "Quarantine" on the door and forbade anyone to enter except members of the immediate family. Johnny got well. None of the other children got diphtheria.

At times his father disappeared for months. No one knew his whereabouts. He fell completely short of being a good father. His mother died when Johnny was 14.

One of 13 children, Johnny was left an orphan. In order to earn money to help support his younger brothers and sisters, he left school to work as a messenger boy and at whatever odd jobs he could find. He was determined to complete high school, and managed to complete his education at night. Several of the children went to an orphanage and others were old enough to go to work. Matt Zadalis, his closest boyhood friend, persuaded his family to take Johnny in, and he lived with them for five years.

  This interview with Matt Zadalis provides an interesting picture of Johnny Goodman's early years. Matt is a retired golf professional living in Omaha, Nebraska. At the time of this writing, he was 87 years old. His son is also a golf professional at the Shoreline Country Club in Carter Lake, Iowa.

AUTHOR - HOW DID YOU GET TO KNOW JOHNNY?

  When his mother died and he was left an orphan, my mother, who was a good friend of Johnny's mother, took him into our family. I was a good friend of Johnny's before that, and a couple of years younger than him. He lived with us for about five years. We remained friends for the rest of his life.

  He was later taken in by the Webster family here in Omaha on the condition that he be responsible for the furnace fire during the winter months.

WHAT WERE THE WINTERS LIKE IN OMAHA?

  Well, winters started early in November and usually lasted through March - not much golf then. In the fall of the year at the Omaha Field Club they would cover the greens and set up temporary sand greens. We used to sneak out there that time of year and play as often as we could in the evenings. Later when Johnny became a tournament winner he was given a membership at that club.

HOW DID YOU BOTH GET INTERESTED IN GOLF?

One day we were walking along the railroad tracks near our home. The tracks bordered the Omaha Field Club. We found a ball that a player had hit onto the tracks and returned it to him. He gave us each a nickel to buy an ice cream cone. He told us we ought to go to the Caddie Master at the club and apply for a job caddying, and we did. Then we started caddying there. Johnny was only 11 years old when his caddie career started. He turned his earnings of 50 cents a day over to his mother.

HOW DID YOU GET YOUR FIRST GOLF CLUB?

Over a few weeks Johnny and I managed to find about 100 golf balls. We presented them to the golf pro, and in return he gave us an old left-handed wooden-shafted mashie (5 iron). There was a dairy farm near our house and we used to hit balls there. We would hit balls and mark the spot where the ball landed. The one who hit the ball the farthest would get to use the club the following week and practice with it.

DID THEY LET THE CADDIES PLAY AT THE OMAHA FIELD CLUB?

Yes, we got a chance to play 9 holes on Mondays. After a while we managed to get enough old clubs, about 6 or 7, that we played with.

WAS JOHNNY A GOOD GOLFER THEN?

Oh yes. When he was 16 years old his friends amongst the members persuaded him to play in the City Amateur Championship. He was afraid his shabby clothes wouldn't look good, so his friends gave him a new golf outfit and this got him to agree to play. He won the tournament, and we were all pleased.

In the first 9 holes he was allowed to play at the club he shot a 37 - he practiced his game a lot and was smart enough to imitate the good golfers he caddied for. He developed a typical caddy swing, short and compact - not much chance for error. He was the champ amongst the caddies.

DID JOHNNY WORK ANYWHERE OTHER THAN THE GOLF COURSE IN THE SUMMER?

Yes. One summer while in high school he worked in the cattle packing house here in Omaha. As to high school, he had to walk about three miles to get there; that didn't bother him because he really wanted to get an education.

At the packing house that summer he worked ten hours a day, six days a week. He earned 30 cents an hour. I remember when he'd get home, he sure smelled awful.

WHAT DO YOU REMEMBER ABOUT JOHNNY'S GAME FROM ALL OF THE YEARS YOU PLAYED GOLF WITH HIM?

He was steady off the tee. In his prime he hit it about 240 yards and seldom missed a fairway - pretty good for what we had to play with then. He had a good compact swing - a strong lower body movement. He favored a draw shot off the tee.

He was the master of the niblick (9 iron). Of course they didn't have wedges or sand wedges then. From 110 to 120 yards into the green he was deadly accurate. The strongest part of his game was chipping and putting - he spent a lot of time practicing those shots.

On the mental side - he was able to completely

focus on his game while he played. He wasn't much for small talk while he played - all business. When he hit a bad shot he wouldn't let it rattle him.

WERE YOU SURPRISED AT JOHNNY'S ACCOMPLISHMENTS IN GOLF?

Yes, I was. He sure had to overcome some real obstacles. He was a determined guy, and I give him a lot of credit. I'm glad he was my friend, and we're all proud of his accomplishments.

An important event in Johnny's life was when Walter Hagen, one of the great American professional tournament golfers of the time, came to Omaha for an exhibition. He asked for "the best boy in the shop" to caddie for him, and they gave him Johnny Goodman. This experience was an inspiration to Goodman. In his wildest imagination he never dreamed that one day in the United States Open he would outplay Hagen.

Since that day when he captured the trophy in his first adult tournament and thus became the youngest city golf champion Omaha had ever had, the name of Johnny Goodman has had a definite meaning to Omaha and Nebraska. It has meant a freckle-faced little fellow with a broad and ready smile. It meant hard work and determination. It meant, above all, excellent golf. Following his remarkable performance in the city tournament, friends of Goodman saw to it that he got a good enough job to enable him to return to high school. And during that summer Johnny went to night school, made up the work he had lost by dropping out the previous winter, and finished his junior year's work when the summer of 1926 rolled around.

He started the season by leading his South High

golf team to victory in the city high school tournament. In so doing, he broke a course record Walter Hagen established several years before at the Dundee links. The figure was a 70 over a par 76 course. Next on the Omaha golf calendar for 1926 came the city tournament in which Johnny was to defend his title. He won medalist honors but lost the championship. In the Nebraska State Tournament, played at Lakewood Country Club Course in Omaha, he was also the medalist. Here, again, he lost an early match and never reached the finals.

Then he went to his first Trans-Mississippi Tournament, representing the Omaha Field Club, which had given him a membership. The tournament was played that year at St. Louis. Johnny with Jack Pollard and Frank Siedlik, two other Omaha youngsters who had been shooting in the low 70's, were unable to afford railroad fare. But that was a matter of small consequence to three teenaged golfers who really wanted to play in the big event of the Midwest. They "shipped out" as drovers to St. Louis, each with a consignment of cattle.

Arriving a few days later at the Algonquin Club, they found themselves a center of interest almost from the start. The sports writers dubbed them as "The Cattle-Car Threesome" and "The Boxcar Trio." Unfettered by the publicity, they appeared on the first tee clad in overalls and the grime of the trip. Johnny surprised the gallery on the first tee when he carried his driver to a bare spot on the tee and rubbed the grip in the dirt - his way of ensuring he had a good grip. All three qualified. Goodman and Pollard worked their way to the semifinals. Both lost; Goodman to John Dawson of Chicago and Pollard to Eddie Held. Young Siedlik won the championship consolation prize.

33

The Boxcar Trio: (From Left) Jack Pollard, Johnny Goodman, and Frank Siedlik

Loaded with honors (the home folks considered them great successes even though they weren't champions) "The Boxcar Trio" returned to work and to school. Johnny, it may be mentioned here, was no longer a caddie and as a result spent less time on the golf course. As a caddie he could not retain his amateur status and play in tournaments. He was working downtown doing odd jobs and paying for his own board and room in a humble house in South Omaha. He was only able to practice golf after work and on Sundays. It meant walking two miles from his lodging to the golf course. At the end of the summer he began his senior year in South High School, making good marks throughout the school year.

I don't think there is any question that the tremendous adversities that Johnny Goodman faced early in his life provided the motivation, almost the obsession, that drove him to reach the upper levels of the world of golf. The really hard knocks he endured toughened him and implanted in his mind and soul a burning desire to succeed. Obviously, he had innate golfing skills, yet surely a lesser person faced with the same obstacles, instead of being challenged would have fallen by the wayside early on. It was this all out desire to win that propelled him throughout his golfing career.

The opening of Goodman's third summer of tournament golf found him just as determined and just as eager to play as he was during the two previous years. A bit more cocky perhaps, but his feet were still on the ground, and the praises and flattery of those first two seasons had slipped lightly off his boyish head. With him, the game was still the uppermost thing. It was an easy matter for him to capture the golf championship of his high school. And the South High team of which he was a member won the city high school team title.

State tournament time came. The event was scheduled for the new Happy Hollow Club links. Once more, Johnny showed among the best by winning medalist honors as he had done the year before in the Nebraska State event. But toward the latter part of the week his game began to slip. Some say it could have been his overconfidence. Whatever the cause, he lost his semifinal match to Foy Porter, a veteran Happy Hollow player who won the championship the following day.

But on the night of his defeat, a defeat that grieved him more than losses in any other tournament, Johnny Goodman graduated from South High School with the goal he so wanted to reach. More than that, he was awarded the top scholarship of two hundred dollars for "citizenship", his fine grades and school spirit. It was a prize which the Omaha World-Herald gave annually to two graduates from each of Omaha's five high schools. This was more than Johnny expected. His sorrow at the loss of the state tournament match was turned to joy, and with a smile of new hope on his face, he doffed his graduation robes, hopped into the automobile of a friend, and sped west to the scene of his next conquest, the Broadmoor Golf Club, in Denver, Colorado.

He entered the 1927 Trans-Mississippi tournament at the age of 18, this time not as a stranger, for he reached the semifinals the previous year. This summer he came to complete the job, to win through the final and take the championship. He started his campaign by turning in the third lowest score for the qualifying rounds, two 76's for 152. Jimmy Manion with 144 and Eddie Held with 149, both former Trans-Mississippi champions, were the only ones who "headed" him. Incidentally, the other two members of "The Boxcar Trio" were there, too. But Pollard had the tough luck to draw Held, the defending champion, in the first round and lost to him, just as he had the year before in the semifinals at St. Louis. And Siedlik, after breezing through the first round, met Manion in the second, and he, too, fell by the wayside.

Of the three, Goodman remained. He fought his way straight through to the semifinals again, where he found himself face to face with the tough little Manion, conqueror of Goodman's comrade. Manion had the advantage both in age and in years of experience. No matter, Johnny was out to win, and win he did, even though it took 38 holes of grueling golf to do it.

Then came the final with James Ward of Kansas City, a man at the very opposite end of life's ladder from that of his young opponent. Ward was a wealthy Kansas City millionaire. He was able to afford the best golf teachers and to spend enough time on the links to work over his game slowly and carefully. He won the Missouri state title and set the tournament record of 68 in an earlier match of this 1927 Trans-Mississippi Tournament. In this he eliminated the doughty Eddie Held in the second round. Unawed, Goodman, the self-made golfer, the lad who won his first big tournament with borrowed clubs and in gift clothes, faced him for the title. He knew there was but one thing to do - play each shot as well as he knew how. How well that was had been proven before. It was proven again when at the end of the first 18 holes of their final match Goodman stood five up on Ward.

But Ward, not discouraged by the margin which was piled against him, came back in the afternoon and fired birdie after birdie at Johnny. At the 32nd green of the match he was only one down. The Omaha youngster, shooting par golf, saw his lead diminished, gritted his teeth, thought of the folks at home and of the title they wanted him to win, and concentrated even harder.

He had the look in his eyes that every true athlete has - a purposeful, dedicated look, reflecting fierce determination. He scored a birdie on the 33rd to go two up, halved the 34th, and then loosed another birdie on the 35th to win the hole and the match three up and one to play. The championship of the Trans-Mississippi Golf Association was his - Johnny Goodman's. He had done it!

Scarcely able to believe his good fortune, Johnny went home to Omaha. This city of some 200,000 had watched Johnny Goodman succeed despite all of the barriers that beset a little fellow determined to overcome his disadvantage. The people of Omaha cheered and applauded as he began to take his place among the golf champions of the city, a golfer self-made through keen observation and conscientious practice. So when Johnny came home after his greatest golf victory, Omaha was ready. The scattered Goodman family was gathered together to welcome the hero brother. Almost all were there - George, Joe, Bill, Tony, Pete, Mike, Anna, and Mary. They were joined by the very proud L. B. Webster family, where Johnny had been making his home that year.

At the outskirts of the city, along the road over which the new golf king was to arrive from Denver, a crowd of 500 friends gathered. When Johnny finally came into sight and drove up to the gathering place, he was given a welcome which approached that of Lindbergh, the great trans-Atlantic flyer. It was real, straight from the heart, a tribute to a boy who had done great things despite great obstacles. Johnny was at first awed by the sight of so many people waiting to meet him. Then, as the shouts of congratulations fell about him and the smiling eyes of his proud brothers and sisters met his, he ducked his head to hide a tear of happiness.

A parade numbering more than a hundred autos, including that of Mayor James Dahlman, traveled through the Omaha streets, followed by a banquet at the Lakewood Club where Johnny belonged (he had been given a membership to this club). Hundreds of golfers and friends attended to offer their proud congratulations. It was the chairman of the Lakewood Executive Committee, Ed Dougherty, and James Sullivan, Secretary of the South Omaha Merchants Association, who arranged for the greeting. As part of the welcome home celebration, an education fund was offered to help Johnny go to college the next fall. Even before Johnny reached home, the subscribed $1,565 ensured his first year at the University of Nebraska, which he entered in 1928.

His roommate at the university, Charley Martin, said he spent a good bit of his time practicing putting on his dormitory room floor and hitting chip shots into the bureau drawer. He left the university at the end of the year. His golf was too much a part of his life, and he was unable to concentrate on academics.

On his return to Omaha, Johnny worked in a sporting goods shop, and then later established a successful insurance agency, selling insurance for Mutual of Omaha to earn a living. That gave him time to devote to developing and honing his golf skills.

Prologue
The Great Depression Era: 1929-1941

Johnny Goodman's golf career spanned most of America's severest economic depression. I think it's helpful to have a brief overview of this period in order to better understand the backdrop of the golfing scene at that time and the context of Johnny Goodman's role in it.

In October 1929 the stock market had crashed and many in the country found themselves with staggering financial losses. What was to follow was a cruel economic depression that spanned the next 12 years.

When Wall Street collapsed and throngs rushed the banks, jobs disappeared, and with them the hopes of a generation. As the depression swept across the country millions of Americans went without food and housing. Poverty was no longer a statistic, it was a commonplace reality.

In 1932 19 million people were jobless. This represented 37.6% of the employable nonfarm population. The unemployed farm population - those people who had to leave their farms - was 25.2%[1]. In some big cities the unemployment rate was as high as 50%. It's an astounding fact that roughly two million Americans - one quarter of a million between the ages of 16 and 21 - were on the road in the year 1932. They were called the "wandering population". Every locality had more welfare cases than it could handle. Impoverished strangers were charged with vagrancy and dumped across the nearest county line. Who were these people? For the most part they were displaced sharecroppers, farmers who had lost their farms because of foreclosed mortgages, and ragged bands of youths graduated from school who couldn't find a job. A high percentage of

[1] *Historical statistics, U.S. Census Bureau*

these people were formerly members of the middle class. Completely new to the experience, they all were nomads of the depression.

In June of 1933, perhaps the worst year of the depression, Ivy League college seniors joined 21,000 other graduating college seniors hunting for a job. By then, elevator operators in New York department stores were required to have a bachelor's degree, and many men with that level of education gladly took such jobs. It was simply the best they could find.

It got so bad that California set up forced labor camps for their poor, and even posted guards on highways entering the state to turn back the poor coming in from other states.

The following is a sample of the annual earnings in 1933 for various occupations. It is difficult to relate to these numbers now, even if they are adjusted for inflation, but they do reveal a lot about the economic situation in those years.

How Much Did We Earn Yearly in 1933?

Waitress	*$520*
Farm hand	*216*
Coal Miner	*723*
Chauffeur	*624*
Seamstress	*780*
Live-in Maid	*260*
Priest	*831*
Typist	*624*
Steelworker	*420*
School teacher	*1,227*
Dentist	*2,391*
Professor	*3,111*
Doctor	*3,382*
Lawyer	*4,218*
Railroad executive	*5,064*
U. S. Congressman	*8,663*

In 1938, 14% of the U. S. population was on welfare, as the depression continued to deepen. Only America's entry into World War II in 1941 ended that cruel depression. The depression had its impact on the world of golf as well. In 1934 alone 283 country clubs shut down completely.

1929

*To keep things in historical perspective,
a look at some of the other outstanding events
that took place that year.*

• Lieutenant James Dolittle (later General Dolittle, who led the air raid against Tokyo, Japan, from an aircraft carrier in World War II and received a congressional medal) was the first to pilot an airplane solely using instruments.

• United States Aviator Richard E. Byrd and three companions fly over the South Pole.

• Herbert Hoover inaugurated as 31st President of the United States.

• Leon Trotsky expelled from the U.S.S.R.

CHAPTER II

Gaining Prominence
In The Golf World -
The National Amateur At
Pebble Beach, California

Earlier in June of the year 1929, Johnny Goodman sprang into prominence by capturing medalist honors among 1,400 amateur and professional golfers competing in the qualifying trials of the United States National Open Tournament. His score of 140 for 36 holes was better than Bobby Jones, Walter Hagen, MacDonald Smith, Gene Sarazen, Leo Diegel, and other fine golfers. The critics applauded but said he was "just a flash in the pan."

At age 20, he was the youngest golfer to qualify for the National Open. A week later he left Omaha for the Winged Foot Course in New York, site of the U.S. Open that year. Because he believed that an amateur should be a real amateur and should not receive financial assistance from anyone, he refused the offers of several Nebraska clubs and journeyed to New York as a steer tender on a cattle train. It would be difficult to imagine a championship golfer traveling like that today.

Johnny Goodman lived by an inspirational message that was written in 1929 by Calvin Coolidge, the President of the United States. Coolidge was elected in 1924, a president who went down in history as an ultraconservative and one who, after he completed his term, refused to run for reelection.

In modern times, that would be an history-making event. Calvin Coolidge was known as " Silent Cal", yet he certainly had a way with words. This is a message that served as Johnny's model:

"Nothing in the world can take the place of persistence. Talent will not; nothing is more common than unsuccessful men with talent. Genius will not; unrewarded genius is almost a proverb. Education will not; the world is full of educated derelicts. Persistence and Determination alone are omnipotent. The slogan 'Press on' has solved and always will solve the problems of the human race."

Critics were not surprised, but Johnny was greatly disappointed when he failed to set the world on fire at the difficult Winged Foot Club in Westchester County, New York. He made the 36 hole cut, but finished in a tie for 45th place with a 72 hole score of 318. Johnny returned to Omaha, disconsolate, but determined to try again.

In September 1929, he set out for the National Amateur at the famous Pebble Beach Course in California. It was there that Johnny first attracted national attention. He arrived at the tournament site again after chaperoning a carload of cattle from Omaha, Nebraska. A friend in Omaha got him a pass as a cattle herder, and he rode in the caboose of the train to Salinas, California, near Pebble Beach.

Because Goodman had been working as a salesman for a sporting goods store, his eligibility for amateur standing was questioned by the officials of the USGA. In no way had he capitalized on his golf skills even though he held the job for some time. Johnny Dawson, who also worked for a sporting goods store, was cross-examined, and he withdrew from the championship. Somewhat the same pressure was exerted on Goodman, but he refused to see how his amateur standing was affected in any way and insisted upon playing, demonstrating his determination and a willingness to stand up for himself.

For years on end, in amateur golf there had been only one supreme name: Robert Tyre Jones, of Atlanta, Georgia, was hailed everywhere as the outstanding golfer of all times. After waiting many years to see the king of golf, the Pacific coast had only a fleeting glimpse of him because of a young golfer named Johnny Goodman.

The name of Jones and the name of Goodman were both on the list of qualifying round survivors and, in the draw, Bobby and Johnny were thrown together for the first round of the match play. Johnny Goodman, at 20, was in his first national amateur test, facing the most formidable opponent of them all, the man who usually vanquished the entire field. In 14 years of competition, Jones had never been defeated in the first round of play. In June of the same year Bobby Jones had won the U.S. Open for the third time.

Pebble Beach
Par For The Course - 72
6,799 Yards

Hole	Yards	Par	Hole	Yard	Par
1	373	4	10	426	4
2	502	5	11	384	4
3	388	4	12	202	3
4	327	4	13	392	4
5	166	3	14	565	5
6	516	5	15	397	4
7	107	3	16	402	4
8	431	4	17	209	3
9	464	4	18	548	5
	3,274	36		3,525	36

The Pebble Beach Course was set up in traditional USGA fashion with tight fairways, deep penalizing rough, and lightning fast and undulating greens. The premium was on accuracy and putting skills. From my inquiry of knowledgeable people, the course has changed very little to the present day except for its present magnificent condition.

Jones' name was known to millions during the so-called Golden Age of Sports, otherwise adorned by Babe Ruth, prizefighting's Jack Dempsey, tennis' Bill Tilden, and professional golf's Walter Hagen. Through his conquests in the British Isles, as well as in this country, he was an international figure and a most popular one at that.

At Pebble Beach that year he was the magnet for record galleries. People came from all over just to see him stroke a golf ball. In a day before motels lined the roadsides, accommodations were virtually unobtainable. In Monterey and Carmel, towns near the site of the Pebble Beach course, all available lodgings had been snapped up weeks in advance. Even so, the swarms kept coming. On the day the tournament started, the narrow road from Salinas to the coast was jammed with cars.

High rollers took over the Del Monte Lodge and the beautiful old Del Monte Hotel, where the rates were $12 a day (a large sum of money for a night's lodgings in 1929) and the American plan menu allowed one the opportunity of ordering four different kinds of melons for breakfast. Unable to reach a decision, many guests settled for all four of them at no extra charge. True, the Depression was only weeks away, but until it arrived there was good living. It was one of those rare times, possibly the last, when money was both plentiful and valuable.

The Calcutta Pool on the tournament was one of the largest ever. Tens of thousands of dollars were poured into it, with the heavy money riding on Jones, the defending champ. In straight betting, Jones was at least 25 to 1 to beat his opening round opponent.

Chill and ominous fog gathered over Pebble Beach, obscuring California's famous golden climate. Several thousand spectators were on hand to view the play at the Pebble Beach Course. Most of them followed the Jones - Goodman match, expecting to see the veteran Georgian give his eager young rival a sound trouncing. Except for the first two holes and the 13th and 14th, Jones played great golf, but those holes were his undoing.

Overall in the match Jones easily outdistanced Goodman from the tees. But the little guy, who didn't know where his caddy fees would come from, kept his shots right down the middle and he was a demon with his putter.

Bobby's ball had a poor lie on the first. He fluffed the shot and was 30 feet short of the green. On the second, he took a six by driving into a bunker, playing out short of the cross bunkers, and eventually became stymied, a position when the ball nearer the hole lies in the line of play of another ball. Goodman, in the same bunker on his drive, just managed to carry the cross bunker on his third and won the hole by chipping up close.

Goodman won the third with a birdie three, holing a 12-foot uphill putt, and so was three up after the first three holes. This was before champion Bobby Jones' breakfast had settled. Johnny, putting better than Jones, showed no fear of the veteran golfer.

Bobby stemmed the tide running so strongly against him by winning the fourth with a birdie three, and he also won the sixth with a birdie four.

Jones' first putting lapse came when he three-putted the short seventh from 20 feet, running four feet past when he went after a birdie. He won the next hole when Goodman's second went into the sand, and he failed to get out on his first attempt.

After that, Bobby began to play real golf, but Goodman never wavered, halving the ninth and tenth with fours and the 11th with a birdie three. Johnny used against Bobby the very philosophy he had learned from his reading of

Bobby's book, "Down The Fairway" - play against "Old Man Par" and not your opponent.

Goodman hung on as tenaciously as a bulldog. He was a fierce competitor who believed he could beat anyone. He carried the greatest golfer of them all to the 17th and had him one down. He decided he would not let his victory and his chance for fame slip through his fingers by losing heart.

On the 18th hole, a par five of 548 yards, Goodman was one up. Both had good tee shots. Jones' second shot was pushed to the right and hit a tree, luckily bounding back into the fairway. Johnny's third, a pitch shot to the green, flew straight toward the flagstick, but it was a little too strong, running up on the back edge of the green and leaving him with a tricky downhill putt. Jones' third, a pitch shot to the green, was 35 feet from the hole.

Jones was away and had to putt first; he had to sink the putt to tie the match. There was utter silence in the huge gallery as he lined up the putt. It seemed doubtful that the ball would reach the hole when it left the face of the putter, then it rolled on and on, straight for the cup. In the last few inches it curled off and stopped beside the hole, just a trifle short and slightly off line.

Goodman now could lose the hole only by taking three putts, and he was determined not to do that. His was a difficult putt, but he rolled his ball down within a foot or so of the hole and then tapped it in. The crowd roared! A rookie golfer had defeated Bobby Jones. He was only the second man to do that in the last five championships. Goodman reached for Bobby's extended hand.

Life Magazine entitled its article about this historic golfing event "The Defeat of Bobby Jones" - "A Painting for Life by William C. Palmer." The painting referred to was one of a series of dramatic scenes in 20th Century American history on commission from *Life Magazine*. It depicts Jones and Goodman on the 17th green at Pebble Beach with Goodman one up and one to play.

Highlighted in *The New York Times* the event was headlined, "Omaha Court Cheers Goodman, Judge Leading Demonstration." The article read: "Omaha had its hour of intense golf enthusiasm this afternoon when the news was flashed that Johnny Goodman, Omaha home-bred, had defeated Bobby Jones. The feeling of high joy seemed to have its centre in the United States Court where Judge Woodrough sits. When the news reached the court room Judge Woodrough jumped to his feet and gave three cheers in which all joined. Judge Woodrough is president of the Lakeside Country Club, which Goodman represented in the tournament."

History was being made that year. Jones was beaten most spectacularly in a first round match for the U. S. Amateur Championship. The day before, the Dow-Jones stock market index hit 381.17, its all-time high. Tilden, the great tennis player that summer had won his last American championship. Babe Ruth was getting older, and Dempsey and Tunney had each fought a last championship fight. The most glorious sporting cycle in world history was drawing to a close. An historical note: two months after that September afternoon the stock market crashed and prosperity came to an end.

Bobby Jones was not as perturbed about his defeat by Johnny Goodman as a lot of his friends and spectators were who followed him to the clubhouse. "We can't win all the time," he said. "I didn't do so well today. The clubs weren't working. We had a great match, though, and Goodman is a fine golfer and a game boy."

Goodman showed the strain he had been under. "Naturally, I got a thrill out of beating Bobby Jones," he said. "Not many are beating him these days. After the first tee I didn't think of anything except winning. I thought I had him on the 17th when I had him one down and missed my putt to close out the match, but I knew my putt was off line the minute I hit it."

Johnny Goodman (left) and the defeated Bobby Jones
during the National Amateur,
Pebble Beach, California, in September 1929

Goodman's win, as proven later by his record of achievement, was not a fluke. Bobby Jones was a spectator at the 1933 U.S. Open when Goodman won and he remarked that perhaps "now people will quit asking me how Goodman beat me at Pebble Beach."

In his next match that same afternoon at Pebble Beach, Goodman was defeated, and thus eliminated, by William Lawson Little, an 18-year-old San Franciscan. Little went on to win the National Amateur and the British Amateur back to back in 1934 and 1935. However, in this tournament, Little was eliminated the next day by Francis Ouimet.

While Omaha doubtless regarded Johnny Goodman a prime hero, California considered him a painful accident that came over two thousand miles to happen. Bobby Jones was defending champion and had been in the previous year, as well. It's little wonder his fans were dismayed. With Jones out of it, thousands of people packed up and left as the area's innkeepers watched their anticipated profits go with them.

In many ways, the defeat of Jones was an important event for golf. It opened up the championship for the first time in five years. Goodman's victory, earned without any flaw or fluke, gave new inspiration to thousands of young golfers, just as Ouimet's victory in the U. S. Open over Varden and Ray did 16 years earlier. This defeat of Jones by Goodman in no way diminished the true greatness of Bobby Jones in the world of golf.

Jones had never lost in the first round of the Amateur before. In the 36-hole pre-qualifying round prior to the match, Jones was tied for medalist, obviously playing really good golf before meeting Johnny Goodman.

Jones' defeat was looked upon as a tragedy by many, as he was the drawing card and the player everyone wanted

52

Bobby Jones congratulating Johnny on his victory

to see, while his opponent was an unknown. "I'm proud," said young Johnny Goodman, "but I'm sorry some people said it was a good thing for the game." This reflected Johnny's great admiration of Bobby Jones. The world remembered only the headline:

UNKNOWN DEFEATS JONES, ONE UP

and came to know and admire the young "unknown" Johnny Goodman.

They came to know, too, that he was a poor boy, orphaned early in life. Thousands of caddies took him as their model.

On his return home, he was given a life membership in the Field Club of Omaha. For having defeated Bobby Jones in 1929 alone, Johnny Goodman would hardly be but a footnote in the history of golf. It's only his achievement in golf thereafter that places him among the great golfers.

The following is an interview with Johnny Goodman's nephew, Jack Atkins, who lives in Omaha, Nebraska. Jack knew Johnny well and played quite a bit of golf with him throughout his life. In fact, he indicated that Johnny "started him in golf" when he (Jack) was a boy of eight.

AUTHOR - WHAT ARE SOME OF THE INTERESTING THINGS YOU REMEMBER ABOUT JOHNNY?

One day on the way to the golf course I asked him "why don't you have a radio in your car?" He replied: "When I'm on the way to play golf, to play a radio would distract from my concentration on the way, for it's then that I concentrate on golf and how I will play when I get there." His ability to concentrate on the golf course was remarkable. He was a very modest fellow. I remember him giving most of his golf trophies to relatives and friends, never keeping any at his place. He made light of his accomplishments and had a self-deprecating sense of humor.

WHAT ARE SOME OF THE COMMENTS HE MADE WHEN HE RETURNED FROM PEBBLE BEACH AND DEFEATING BOBBY JONES?

He told me something very few people know. He said: "I was sitting next to Bing Crosby the great entertainer at the banquet for the players on Sunday evening. Crosby lived next to the golf course and even then was a great golf enthusiast. He was very pleasant to me and congratulated me on my win against Jones and said he thought I had a good future in golf. He invited me to stay over and play a match with him the next day. I agreed, but I had trouble sleeping that night knowing that I would be playing golf with such a celebrity. He insisted on making a wager on the match, which I was reluctant to do. Crosby was a pretty fair golfer, yet I felt confident that with the way I was playing I would win, which I did. Crosby said that he thoroughly enjoyed playing with me even though I won the match by a wide margin. He congratulated me on my victory, and when we parted wished me a safe trip home. He couldn't have been any nicer to me than he was. He followed my career over the years and we became lifelong friends."

Another comment he made after returning from Pebble Beach was: "You know I was the most hated man in California for beating Bobby Jones - the people who came to watch Jones play and missed out on seeing him wanted to know who in the hell was that damn kid that kicked Jones out of that tournament."

Johnny was a survivor and I think his adversity led to his achievements. He embodied all the qualities of the underprivileged kid who wanted to succeed.

*Johnny Goodman with his friend, movie star,
and avid golfer, Bing Crosby*

A Round of Golf With
Johnny Goodman Today

I'd like to take you on a round of golf I played in my imagination with Johnny Goodman. This was the year 1929, just after he defeated Bobby Jones at Pebble Beach.

First of all, it was nice of Johnny to agree to play a round with me. I just wanted to show him our modern high-tech golf equipment, for I was sure he would appreciate it all.

As we started out, I couldn't help notice the way Johnny was dressed - a shirt and tie and a drab pair of knickers, no golf glove. I noticed his shoes looked like street shoes that someone had put spikes in as an afterthought. I felt a little out of place with my Greg Norman straw hat, Brooks Brothers golf shirt, doeskin golf glove, silk slacks, and waterproof Foot Joy golf shoes - everything color coordinated.

I told Johnny I wanted to ride in a golf cart, as I always do, but he insisted on walking. How old-fashioned can you get?

He gave me the honors, which I thought was generous of him. I teed up my Great-Flight, low trajectory Z-Balata two-piece ball and pulled out my Big Brother titanium head, graphite-shafted driver with its stability weighted systems and high performance grip. All of this, I was promised, would give me greater distance from an effortless swing. Johnny just stared at my driver, but didn't say a word. I managed to get it in the fairway and was pleased with my start.

Johnny pulled out his driver, and I couldn't believe it. It had a wooden head and, of all things, wooden shaft. He took very little time and just whacked what looked like a drugstore type golf ball a long way down the center of the fairway.

He didn't change his ball every three holes and go to a new ball like the pros do. I guess the poor kid couldn't afford to.

We strode down the fairway with our caddies. His golf bag was just big enough to carry his eight clubs and a few golf balls. How he ever played without rain gear, towels, high energy granola bars, a dozen or two golf balls, and the like, is more than I can understand. During the round, I couldn't help but notice the way he stared at my golf bag filled with clubs that were perimeter weighted, maximum forgiveness, titanium heads with extra long graphite shafts. My golf bag was big enough to carry both he and his clubs.

On his second shot, he didn't pull out a yardage chart like I did. Neither did he consult at length with his caddy. Maybe that was because he was a caddy once himself. He hit his second shot with a club called a spoon. Amazing how well he hit it with such a crude looking club.

When we got to the green, he didn't mark his ball and have it cleaned by his caddie before he putted. I'll be darned if he didn't touch his ball at all. He looked on in amazement as I repaired all the ball marks on the line of my putt, had my caddy clean my ball, place it and then proceeded to plumb-bobb. On one occasion when I had my caddie stand behind me to line up my putt, he looked like he wanted to say something, but resisted out of politeness. He took very little time putting and almost acted like he just didn't care. Despite all of this, he did have a lot of one-putt greens, where the ball went into the cup dead center.

At the end of nine holes, I dug into my bag for a

snack, a couple of Power Bars, athletic energy food, fuel for optimum performance. I offered one to Johnny, and he said he didn't think he needed one.

I must say, he was a pretty darn good golfer, for I lost hole after hole. He was very nice about it all, consoling me by saying that I just must be having one of those bad days that happens on occasion to all golfers.

During the round when my ball was bunkered, I, of course, used my dynamite sand wedge, and I had the feeling that he was looking admiringly at that club, and I was tempted to let him use it. When he was in a bunker, which was seldom, he pulled out a niblick, wooden-shafted, of course, and always managed to hit it close to the flagstick.

When I used my "L" wedge on my approach shot Johnny was especially impressed, even though the ball did go to the left in a bunker. He hit his wooden-shafted niblick, the only one he carried, and knocked it past the flagstick and it spun back to within two feet of the hole. It had to have been a lucky shot.

On the next to the last hole, I did manage to tie him on a short par three. When we finished the round, Johnny was very gracious, and I thanked him for the experience. He didn't say a word about the display of high-tech golf equipment I threw at him but, in his heart, I bet he wished he had been born a whole lot later.

1932

Some of the outstanding historical events
that took place that year:

• The Yankees won the World Series in four
straight games against the Chicago Cubs.

• The Tomb of the Unknown Soldier
dedicated in Arlington National Cemetery.

• Franklin D. Roosevelt defeated Hoover
for the presidency in a landslide victory.

• Stalin's wife died; suicide suspected.

• Colonel Charles Lindbergh's baby kidnapped.

The National Amateur 1932, at the Five Farms Course, Baltimore, Maryland. Francis Ouimet, one of golf's greatest, Captain of the Walter Cup Team and Champion the previous year, congratulates Johnny Goodman who defeated him in the quarter finals, 4 and 2.

CHAPTER III

Johnny Goodman's Play in the Years Following Pebble Beach

In 1932 Johnny Goodman became a "cause celebre" when he was snubbed and left off the Walker Cup Team. It may be unfair to say this, but I think one of the reasons Johnny was not chosen for the prestigious Walker Cup Team involved the fact that he didn't have the polish or the sophistication or the rhetoric that was acceptable to the higher circles of society then.

In 1932 he won the gold medal for being low amateur in the U. S. Open played at Fresh Meadows Country Club in Flushing, N.Y. He tied for 14th and had a final round of 68. Gene Sarazen was the winner that year with Bobby Cruickshank being runner up.

That same year he got his revenge by beating four Walker Cup Team members on his way to the National Amateur finals. Finally, he was selected for the 1934 Walker Cup Team, only after his victory in the 1933 U.S. Open.

On September 17, 1932, Johnny Goodman went to the finals in the National Amateur at the Five Farms Course in Baltimore, Maryland, losing two and one to C. Ross Somerville of Canada. This was one of the greatest contests in the history of the U.S. Amateur. In reaching the finals, Goodman eliminated H. Chandler Egan, Charles

Seaver, Maurice J. McCarthy, and Francis Ouimet. Each
of the players was a Walker Cup player. Egan and Ouimet
were two-time National Amateur champions.

Now I'll describe Johnny's play in the finals of
the 1932 National Amateur. C. Ross Somerville, the
ultimate winner, was a 29-year-old insurance actuary from
London, Ontario, the first Canadian to take our National
Amateur Havemeyer Cup to Canada. For that, he was a
real Canadian hero. Johnny Goodman, the 23-year-old
insurance salesman from Omaha, Nebraska, opposed him.
Goodman carried the winner to the 35th hole of the 36-
hole match before losing two and one.

The match was a thrilling struggle all the way.
Played on a cool, windy day, the truly championship course
was set up to usual high USGA standards. Somerville was
a long driver. With the wind on one hole, one of his drives
traveled over 300 yards. He out drove Goodman as much
as 30 yards on many holes. Johnny was not a long hitter
off the tee, but what he lacked in distance, he made up for
with lots of savvy and dogged determination. Also,
Goodman's fine short game kept him alive throughout. Both
played their irons superbly - midirons, mashie niblicks, and
niblicks were the order of the day.

Goodman seldom talked on the course, preferring
to concentrate on his game. Interestingly, he was matched
with an even more taciturn opponent, C. Ross Somerville.
Goodman mentioned that he said "Good putt" to him five
times, and all Somerville replied was "Thank you."

In the afternoon they were all even at the end of
the 29th hole. Somerville won the 388 yard par four 30th
hole when Goodman hit his second shot, a mid-iron, into
the bunker short of the green and came out three feet short
of the hole. Somerville's second was ten feet above the
hole. He two putted, while Goodman missed his short

but difficult putt. Now Goodman was one down. On the 33rd, a 425 par four hole, both parred, still leaving Somerville one up.

The 34th hole was critical. It was a 402 yard par four hole to a small green, requiring a very accurate second shot. Somerville hit a big drive of 270 yards to the center of the fairway and a delicate pitch shot to within 12 feet of the flagstick. Goodman was on the fringe with his second, and then chipped within three feet of the hole. Somerville sank his difficult putt with a smooth, controlled stroke for a birdie. Somerville now two up with two to play.

On the 35th hole, a 155-yard par three, Somerville was on the green nicely, while Goodman was short in the rough. He knew he had to sink his next shot to stay alive. He knocked it stone dead to one foot from the flagstick. Somerville then putted to within inches of the hole.

Goodman, realizing it was over, graciously walked over and shook the hand of the winner. There was a roar from the gallery. Goodman, the giant killer, had been beaten two up on the 35th hole.

In reaching the finals that year, Goodman did have the satisfaction of a close match. He was pleased that on the way to the finals he had beaten Francis Ouimet, one of golf's greatest and captain of the Walker Cup Team that year. Despite this and other accomplishments, he was denied, for reasons known only to the selectors, a place on the Walker Cup in 1932.

In the early spring of 1933, Johnny had an interesting experience as recalled by Charlie Yates, during a personal interview I had with him. Yates himself was one of the fine amateur golfers of that era. He is now 84 years old, but remembers Johnny as a "special friend". In the course of his amateur golf career, Yates won the 1938

British Amateur, the 1935 Western Amateur, and was a member of the 1936 and 1938 Walker Cup Teams, playing team matches along side Johnny Goodman. Yates was also the low amateur in the Masters five times - a man with a superb record.

Johnny was traveling south from Omaha in his old car early in the spring of 1933, searching for warmer weather in which to practice his game before the U. S. Open. His car broke down in Atlanta, Georgia, where a friend he had made during the 1932 National Amateur - Charlie Yates - lived. At the time, Yates was attending Georgia Tech University, and played on their golf team. Johnny called him for help, and then ended up staying at Yates' home for the next three weeks.

During Johnny's stay he and Charlie became very good friends and played golf together every day at the East Lake Course in Atlanta, the home course of Bobby Jones. Charlie said:

"As soon as I got out of class at Georgia Tech, Johnny and I were on the course. We really hit it off just being together. Johnny had a good sense of humor, and was just a regular kind of guy. He had plenty of confidence in his game, but was still pretty modest. He was accurate off the tee and extremely accurate with his irons, with an amazing short game. With the caliber of his play, I wasn't the least bit surprised when he won the National Open that year. I considered Johnny to be one of my best friends, and despite his lack of university education, he could hold his own in anyone's company."

*Johnny Goodman - December 1933 - low amateur in
the Miami-Biltmore Tournament*

1933

Again, to keep things in perspective, let's take a look back at some interesting things that happened that year:

• Primo Carnera knocks out Jack Sharkey to win the heavyweight boxing crown.

• All books by non-Nazi and Jewish authors burned in Germany.

• Adolph Hitler appointed German Chancellor.

• National Amateur Golf Tournament won by George Dunlap.

CHAPTER IV

Winning The Premier Golf Event:
The 1933 United States Open Golf Tournament At The North Shore Links in Glenview, Illinois

One needs to bear in mind that the United States Open, the winning of which was the highlight of Johnny Goodman's career, is the premiere event in the world of golf in the United States. It's the ultimate test of skill for the golfer. Football has its Super Bowl, baseball the World Series, but for golf the tournament of all tournaments is the United States Open. Now on to the exciting story of this event.

The North Shore Links, while decidedly flat, was an excellent test of golf skills, so far as shot making goes. Every club in the bag came into play at one time or another. It was 6,927 yards long with a par of 72 with the usual USGA narrow fairways and wrist-breaking, roughs. Yet, the course was a fair test of championship golf. One pro joked that the fairways were so narrow you had to pass through them single file. The greens were very undulating and as slick as a bald man's head. The course record, a 69, was held by Al Espinosa.

Seldom has there been a championship held in more searing hot weather than it was that year. On the first day, the temperature was close to 100 degrees - a real heat wave in progress.

There is no question that after Jones' grand slam in 1930 and his subsequent retirement from competitive golf at the age of 28, the competitive field in golf changed markedly due to his absence. However, the field was strong for the Open. The finest professionals and amateurs of the day were playing. Just a few of the great players were: Gene Sarazen, defending champion and four-to-one favorite to win, Walter Hagen, Tommy Armour, Craig Wood, Paul Runyan, and Ralph Guldahl.

The North Shore Links
Par For The Course - 72
6,927 Yards

Hole	Yards	Par	Hole	Yards	Par
1	439	4	10	446	4
2	489	5	11	349	4
3	167	3	12	552	5
4	447	4	13	185	3
5	353	4	14	375	4
6	421	4	15	511	5
7	536	5	16	160	3
8	229	3	17	423	4
9	408	4	18	437	4
	3,489	36		3,438	36

On the second day of the tournament, with most of the gallery following him, Goodman started the round four-three-two (a par, an eagle, and a birdie). Goodman was by nature quiet and single-minded and didn't communicate with the gallery, yet his golf was a pure joy to watch. Like Ben Hogan, Goodman said little while he played. He was out to win and didn't want to disturb his concentration by engaging in social banter. He had the right blend of patience, aggressiveness, and intelligence to win the Open. He was able to accept bad breaks as a part of the game. He had the reputation among his competitors of being a good sportsman, whatever the outcome.

Coming to the last hole, needing a birdie for a 66, a score never made by an amateur in either the National Amateur or National Open championship, Goodman cracked a drive on the 18th hole that hugged the left side of the fairway a bit too closely. When his ball stopped, half of it was in the rough and half out. Taking a five iron, he hit the ball cleanly.

When the ball left the club head, there was doubt whether it would reach the green, approximately 170 yards away. It had tremendous overspin coming out of the rough, however, and kept on rolling until it stopped three feet to the right of the hole. He coolly tapped it in for his birdie three. The fantastic score of 66 in the second round at North Shore Links, which broke Espinosa's record 69, effectively earned the Open title for Goodman.

He had only 25 strokes on the greens that day, a brilliant putting round and a spectacular round of golf. Goodman received an ovation from the gallery such to rival that given to Bobby Jones. In the round he hit only 12 greens in regulation, yet he pitched and chipped so well he saved par on the six greens he missed. Driving accurately and well he hit every fairway and reached one par 5 in two.

Following is a graphic record of Johnny's play at each hole and excerpts taken from an account by Charles Bartlett, of *The Chicago Tribune* (Diagrams by William Wallace of Chicago follow the excerpts).

"The Open this year was an affair of marches, counter-marches, upsets, near upsets. The first day Tommy Armour, a lean one-eyed Scot who learned golf

at Edinburgh before the war, the professional who won our Open in 1927 and the British Open in 1931, turned in a card of 68, four under par, to lead the field.

The next day, Tommy Armour slumped to a 75 and Goodman stepped into the lead with the 66 that knocked the breath out of the competition. That 66 was really too much. No one could overtake it.

The pressure attached to holding the lead through two days began to tell on Goodman. Johnny acted as though he had been hit with a left hook when he was in front by a good margin. He was in bunkers and rough, rough and bunkers, and more of the same. Yet, Goodman was the only one of the leaders to stand up under the terrific strain of the crucial third round. He took a six-stroke lead on the field in the morning, by registering a 70. This gave him a total of 211 and paved the way for a record-breaking feat.

In order to lower the 72-hole championship mark of 286, established by Chick Evans at the Open at Minikahda in 1916, and equaled by Sarazen last year he had to score a 74 on his last round in the afternoon. Fully 8,000 spectators, large for those days, attended the closing day of the tournament, focusing their attention almost solely on the young amateur star, Johnny Goodman. They trailed him on both the morning and afternoon rounds of the 36-hole final day, not once deserting him. After he had finished, they set out after Ralph Guldahl, the leader closest to Goodman.

After a brisk lunch of cottage cheese, he got off to a gorgeous start, playing the first three holes in four under par; however, Goodman began to crack under the terrific strain. He went five strokes over par on the last four holes of the outgoing nine, but pulled himself together and scored the last nine in 37, one over par.

It seemed utterly improbable that anyone else in the field would come anywhere near overhauling Goodman. Johnny's 70 had put him six strokes ahead of Ralph Guldahl, seven ahead of Craig Wood, eight in front of Tommy Armour, and nine ahead of Olin Dutra.

The outlook for the Nebraskan's rivals appeared even more dismal when Johnny, playing with MacDonald Smith as a partner, started his final round with a par. (Bear in mind the last day of the Open then was played over 36 holes.) Then he had an eagle three on the second and a birdie two on the third.

At that stage of the tournament all indications pointed to the smashing of the championship record by several strokes. He had par left for the remaining 15 holes for a score of 280.

But suddenly something happened to Goodman's game. He began to waver on the fourth hole where he pushed his second shot wide of the green. He pitched his next two yards beyond the hole and missed the putt, taking a five. No one thought much of that, however, for his lead was so great that he could well afford to lose a stroke occasionally.

But then he lost five shots to par on the last four holes of the outgoing nine. He was bunkered on No. 6, taking his ball out too cleanly and sending it over the green.

Johnny pushed his drive into the rough among the trees on the next hole and pulled his spoon shot into a bunker on the short No. 8. When he was off line in his first two shots to the ninth, the championship appeared to take on a new complexion.

Fortunately for himself, however, Goodman did manage to get back into his stride after passing the turn. On the tenth he succeeded in getting a par four. He later

*said that on the tenth, "I knew if I was going to win I'd
have to play par golf for the rest of the round. I sort of
lost my head when I got that eagle on the second.*

*He got down in two putts on the 11th for a par
four, but had to work for his pars on the next two. Johnny
lost a stroke on the 14th but got it back on the long 15th
where he* had a birdie four.

*It looked like clear sailing until he dropped his
tee shot to the short 16th hole into a bunker. But he
came out and dropped a critical ten-footer for a par three,
a great demonstration of nerve control under pressure.*

*Then, after missing a five-footer on the 17th
green, he played the home hole like a master for par.
However, the best Johnny could do was a 76 for a 72
hole total of 287, one stroke above the all-time record
for the Open.*

*Guldahl, the closest contender, was still out on
the course. His prospects grew brighter as he went along.
He reached the turn in 35, one under par, and closed up
four strokes, leaving him only two shots behind.*

*Picking up four strokes on the Omaha youngster
by playing the first nine of the final round in 35 strokes,
Guldahl, a former Texas amateur, drew even with
Goodman at the end of the 69th hole.*

*He lost a stroke by taking three to get in from the
edge of the green on the next hole, where he failed to
sink a three-foot putt for a four. He regained it two holes
later, however, when he got a birdie three on the 17th
hole.*

*Guldahl thus was faced with the necessity of
getting a birdie three on the home hole to win. A par
four would tie. A tremendous hitter, Guldahl hit a long
drive on the 18th, in perfect position for his second shot
to the green.*

Without spending too much time over the shot, he whipped out an iron. His aim was a trifle to the right and his ball landed on the slope of a bunker guarding the left-hand side of the green bouncing into the sand. He didn't have much green to work with between the edge of the green and the flag stick.

Silence reigned around the green as he went down into the bunker to look over his lie. The young pro, apparently unnerved by the mishap, wiped his hands with a towel.

He seemed to regain his poise as he took his stance to play the shot on which so much was at stake. Finally, he flicked the ball out onto the green, and it started for the hole.

For a moment it appeared as if it would roll dead to the hole but finally it stopped, and Guldahl was left with a putt of not more than four feet. He had to hole it in order to tie Goodman, which would mean a 36-hole play off.

Taking his stance, Guldahl gave the ball a little tap, but he had not figured the slope of the green quite accurately. The ball started for the hole, then curled off. It missed the cup by a slight margin on the left-hand side, inches away.

A look of keen disappointment came over Guldahl's bronzed face as he watched the white ball slide by the side of the hole, carrying with it his chance for the title."

The following three pages are diagrams of Johnny Goodman's second round of 66 at the 1933 U. S. Open. Figures in the lower left-hand corner in each case show the number of the hole, the par, and the length of the hole. In the lower right-hand corner is shown Goodman's score in each case. Figures near the line of the shot indicate the club used for the shot. The driver, of course, was used from the tee on all full-shot holes, and only once did he use his brassie, on the 511 yard 15th. He had ten one-putt greens, and holed a chip shot at the 15th. He three-putted the 11th from 16 feet. He was trapped on three holes, but never missed the fairway once.

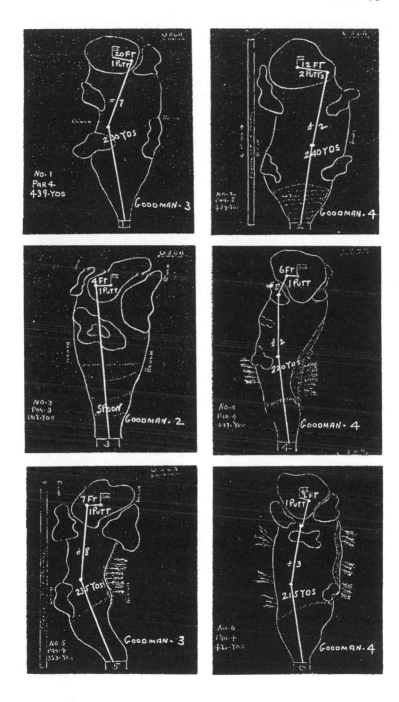

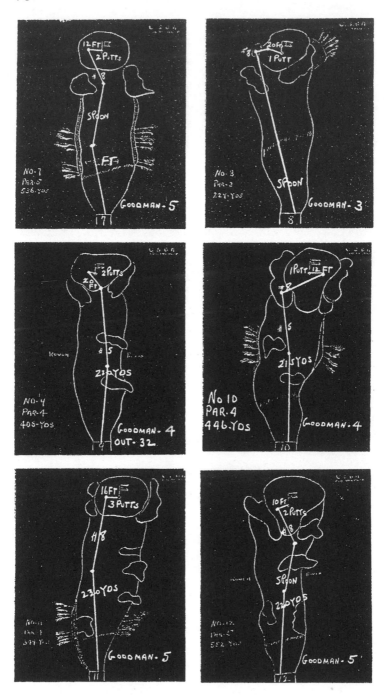

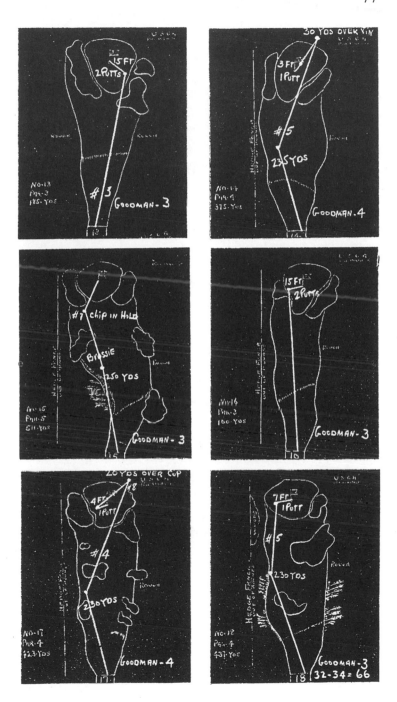

Guldhal took the $1,000 first prize money as the low professional, while Goodman as an amateur received the gold medal as winner. It's interesting to note that the first prize for the winner of the 1996 Open was $425,000.

Here are the top five total scores in the 1933 United States Open Golf Tournament.

Par For 72 Holes - 288

Johnny Goodman, Omaha 75	66	70	76	287
Ralph Guldahl, St Louis.......76	71	70	71	288
Craig Wood, Deal, N.J.........73	74	71	72	290
Walter Hagen, Detroit...........73	76	77	66	292
Tommy Armour, Chicago......68	75	76	73	292

Following are some excerpts from accounts of Grantland Rice, the great sports writer of the past, who was in the gallery at the 1933 United States Open:

"In the latest Open Golf Championship of the United States, played over the narrow fairways of North Shore, Chicago, Johnny Goodman held his own with driver and iron. But in the final summing up, it was his deadly accuracy with chip shots and putts that decided the issue against the gallant counterattacks of Ralph Guldahl and Craig Wood, who almost pinned him down during the run through the finishing stretch.

Guldahl was nine strokes back of Goodman with only 15 holes to go. But at this point Johnny Goodman lost his short game touch, and for the next six holes he was wobbling badly. He was slipping at his strongest point, just off and around the greens. Lapses of this type gave him even fives for the six holes.

As it turned out, Guldahl picked up seven strokes on those six holes from the fourth through the ninth. He caught Goodman at the 14th green. At this stage he had picked up nine valuable strokes on his leading rival in just 11 holes.

It is hard to imagine anyone picking up almost a stroke a hole on an open champion over a stretch of 11 consecutive holes. And yet, that is just what Guldahl did. It all goes to show what can happen in an open championship.

The story began to boil down to the decisive play at the long 15th. This is an account of how they played the same holes at different times. Here Goodman had a good drive and a good second, 30 yards off the green. Guldahl in turn had a fine drive and a great second and just about reached the edge of the green. Because of his greater distance off the tee, Guldahl had a distinct advantage. Goodman laid his chip shot five feet beyond the pin and then holed the putt for a four. Guldahl laid his approach four feet from the cup, and just missed. It was a costly miss.

Guldahl had exactly the same length putt for a tie on the 18th green and the memory of the missed attempt at the 15th must have remained in his subconscious mind, if it was not an actual haunting ghost. The missed putt cost him a tie with Goodman.

Any golfer who sets a smoking pace for 30 holes is usually due for a turn. The keen edge wears away. So outstanding credit is due Johnny Goodman for the brave rally that followed his sinking spell. He was skidding fast. His game was breaking up. It is a terrific burden to know that you have had a big lead shot away, a sure, wide margin blown apart. Few can come back against such a hostile turn of events. Panic usually sets in. But under this strain Goodman played the last four holes in par, and he got his four where he needed it most, on the final green.

Another big feature of this championship was the play of Tommy Armour and Walter Hagen, two seasoned campaigners who can look back across the years to more than one big triumph. They are among the few who have won both the United States and British Open and also the PGA. It is worthy of note that Armour's 68 in a high wind on the first day and Hagen's 66 on the last round stand out as two of the leading features of the tournament. Hagen's great round included two strokes as an out-of-bounds penalty, meaning that he actually holed out on the 18 holes in 64 actual strokes.

The galleries at North Shore were well handled throughout. And few galleries have ever known a longer run of thrills, starting with Tommy Armour's 68 and finishing with the three-cornered fight among Goodman, Guldahl, and Wood, with Hagen supplying a big share of the final fireworks - a 66 with a shot out of bounds for a two-stroke loss.

Goodman deserved his place at the top. He was able to follow a brilliant 66 with a 70 - 136 for two rounds.

This is a blasting pace, for ordinarily 66's are followed by 75's. He also was able to rally on the brink of disaster, a killing disaster with a nine-stroke lead and only 15 holes to go. To have lost under those conditions would have been much tougher than it was for Guldahl to miss that final putt. For even though Guldahl just fell short in his great challenge, his performance should be the source of a great deal of satisfaction to him.

Johnny Goodman has a sound all-around game. He isn't the longest hitter in the world, but he is long enough and consistently straight. He has a rather fast back-swing, at least it is on the fast side, around three-quarters in length. He is a sound, crisp iron player, but

Johnny Goodman putting in the United States Open

Johnny Goodman, on the left,
and Ralph Guldahl, 1933 U. S. Open

his short game is one of the main foundations of his success. He has a smooth, sure, putting stroke that depends largely on wrist action. He is deadly around the four-or-five-foot range, which is so often the nagging distance in a medal play round. And he is cool and confident.

Goodman had to knock in a few putts from an inch or so away, putts he had barely missed. He missed a few that he should have gotten. Goodman's hip action is free and flexible. A study of action pictures will show this plainly. He will be something to watch for a long time to come.

Goodman's fine round of 70 on top of that record-breaking 66 on the third start left him six strokes ahead of the field. Guldahl stepped into the position of runner-up then and there, with a clever 70 for a total of 217, leading Craig Wood by one stroke. Armour had taken a 76 and was fourth at 219.

Doubtless, the flinty veneer which characterized Goodman's demeanor sprang from those years of struggling for existence in the stern school of the caddie corral. He rode the rods with hoboes to his earlier tournaments and tended cattle on a livestock train en route to his first National Open at Winged Foot. Old beyond his 29 years, Johnny had acquired the tough-fibered, hard-shell philosophy which distinguishes the battle-scarred regular army campaigner from the callow volunteer. Golf was a grim ordeal rather than a casual diversion to Goodman. Although an amateur, he had the professional manner in action and was mentally attuned to that grueling test.

In the locker room after he finished his last round, he fretted and fussed and reproached himself for a 'gutless finish.' 'I don't deserve to win after blowing such a lead,' he kept repeating. In golf, only fractions of an inch separate the glamorous champion from the forgotten runner-up.

Johnny Goodman, meanwhile fidgeted restlessly in the locker room alcove, getting recurrent reports of his pursuer's progress. Only an open championship contender can appreciate the long drawn-out torment of waiting and worrying which the early leader endures while his unseen rivals try to match or better those immutable figures on the scoreboard. 'I'm too tired to care what happens,' Goodman mumbled, but his apprehensive glances toward the press tent door and his quivering fingers belied those words. The boy who had persevered such a superficial mask on the links was near collapse now that he could no longer find relief in physical action.

Johnny's ordeal ended at last as the locker room was stormed by a mob of howling dervishes, yelling - 'He missed the putt, he missed the putt!' They 'chaired' the new champion and carried him 'round the room in a triumphal tour. No Roman conqueror ever drew a more spontaneous ovation, but can you picture one of the Caesars clad in nothing but his porous knit underclothes?"

Following are some interesting comments on Johnny Goodman made by Robert T. Jones, Jr., who was in the gallery at the United States Open in 1933:

"There are always a number of golfers in an Open Championship who happen to be driving well and hitting their iron shots up to standard tests. But there are not so many who can link these two features to a strong short game. I think everyone was impressed with the manner in which Johnny Goodman stepped up to his chip shots

and his putts - he wasted no time or motion in finding the vicinity of the pin or the bottom of the cup.

He stands to the ball well, with his feet fairly close together. He has sound, crisp wrist action on these shorter shots, and he gives you the appearance of being entirely comfortable and quite confident of getting the desired results. He doesn't give himself the chance to get tied up, to absorb tension before he hits the ball. Yet there is nothing hurried or careless in the way he plays these strokes. He gets his line, takes his stance, and then hits the ball.

A fine chip shot can often make up for a bad mistake. Ability to hole most of the four-and-five-foot putts will save many strokes in 72 holes. Missing a few of these putts will make it difficult for anyone to win.

Goodman's tee shots and his iron play were both quite good, but the same could be said of a dozen leading stars. It was his cool, comfortable, confident manner of chipping and putting that turned the trick. He did a fine and workmanlike job in winning."

What kind of a man was Johnny Goodman? Following are some, excerpts from an interview following his 1933 win of the United States Open:

"I never considered myself cocky, if you mean I was a show-off, bragging type player. People may have mistaken confidence for cockiness. Yes, I was a confident player, most of the time, but I don't think anyone can play good golf unless he has a big share of confidence. When I was playing a lot, I played with a lot of confidence, and you can't win any other way. I know I'm going to miss some shots in a round, so I play the rest of the shots the best way I know how.

Confidence is built on repeated success and the memory of success. If I missed a putt, I tried to forget that stroke immediately. Never store up memories of the shots that fail, only the ones that work. And there is one other thing that helped me win there. Never change your style or pace of play. A lot of people will go through a different pre-stroke routine if they face a putt which they feel is a 'must' putt. That is a bad habit. I never felt it helped me to delay stroking a putt after I once had the line and speed figured out. Extra looking doesn't help unless you normally waste time lining up every putt.

No sir, the bigger a stroke is, the more you should approach it just like any other. The fellow who 'tries harder' on a crucial shot is more likely to mess it up."

In 1923 a ragged, barefoot, penniless caddie from the Shantytown section of Omaha, Nebraska, in 1933 a dashing young national idol, champion of all amateur and professional golfers in the United States, became the National Open golf champion.

Winning the championship against such a field, Johnny could have turned professional. In the midst of the Depression, the Open title was financially attractive, but he resisted the change. At the time, he was earning a modest living as an insurance agent. He wanted to remain an amateur primarily because he wanted to emulate his idol, Bobby Jones. He said, "I love the game too much to make it a business." True to these words, Goodman remained an amateur throughout his career.

Timing obviously can mean everything. If Goodman had won the Open as an amateur in 1993 instead of 1933, it doesn't take much imagination to think of how it would have been received by the public. The commercial value alone certainly would have been tremendous. There was no modern-day Mark McCormack to step in and manage him.

As you might have imagined, there was a great parade awaiting Johnny on his return to Omaha. He sat in the open car surrounded by the mayor and governor of Nebraska. He reached down a strong hand to shake the hand of a kid in ragged overalls. A score of urchins surrounded the car and laughed at the efforts of the police to disperse them. This was a dramatic moment; for not so long ago he, himself, was one of the barefoot caddies who fought to shake his hand. In his home town, Goodman was the mighty mite, an institution who had crept closer to Omaha's heart than any of its sons.

Goodman's victory was one of the biggest upsets ever in the U.S.Open. To maintain the level of performance that he did against competition that was as good as it got at that time, was truly extraordinary. You could argue that the competition was not as stiff as it is now. I think, perhaps, that the competition was not as deep, yet facing golfers like Hagen, Armour, Sarazen, and Guldahl proved to be plenty of stiff competition. The professionals were most unhappy for letting an amateur show them up. Eventually, they joined the golfing world in taking their hats off to a boy who stood up to the hard blows of life like a man and overcame barrier after barrier to rise to the top.

Johnny had realized one of his goals, winning the National Open. The other two, becoming a member of the Walker Cup Team and winning the National Amateur, were still part of his dream.

Johnny Goodman, of Omaha, became the fifth amateur in the history of American golf to win the National Open Championship. The only other amateurs besides Goodman who ever won the National title were Francis

Ouimet, Jerome D. Travers, Chick Evans, and Bobby Jones. Ouimet triumphed in 1913, Travers in 1915, Evans in 1916, and Jones in 1923, 1926, 1929, and 1930.

As a postscript to the Open that year, an interesting sidelight provided insight into the personality of the great golfer Walter Hagen. Hagen was as happy over his final round 66 as though he had won the title. His ego expanded visibly. In carnival mood he heard that his arch rival, Gene Sarazen, was somewhere out on the course enmeshed in the cabbage-like rough.

Disgruntled Sarazen, the toast of Fresh Meadow, was hopelessly in the rough. Walter recalled an article, under Gene's signature, implying that an old man like Hagen should be sitting in an armchair instead of playing golf. That insinuation had gotten under Walter's skin. Here was his chance to square accounts. Summoning a bellboy, Hagen paid him five dollars to lug a chair out to where Sarazen was toiling in the sun and to announce, "Your armchair, sir, with the compliments of Walter Hagen."

Gene Sarazen once said of Walter Hagen: "All the professionals who have a chance to win the big money today should say a silent prayer to Walter Hagen. It was Walter who made professional golf what it is."

Another interesting sidelight in that U.S. Open was that Horton Smith, the subsequent winner of the Masters in 1936, finished 12th and won $12.00 as prize money.

Jack Nicklaus came close to winning the National Open as an amateur. He finished second to Arnold Palmer's winning score of 280 at Cherry Hills in 1960 with a score of 282, the lowest score ever posted by an amateur in the U.S. Open.

Another fine amateur who came close to winning the U. S. Open was a 21 year old named Jim Simons during the 1971 U. S. Open, played on the East Course at Merion,

Pennsylvania. Paired with Jack Nicklaus, he was contending with brilliant play, until the 72nd hole where he played himself out of contention. This was the Open that Trevino won in a play off with Nicklaus. Trevino made the humorous remark at the close of play; "I love Merion, and I don't even know her last name."

Johnny Goodman playing from the rough
in his final round of the 1933 U. S. Open

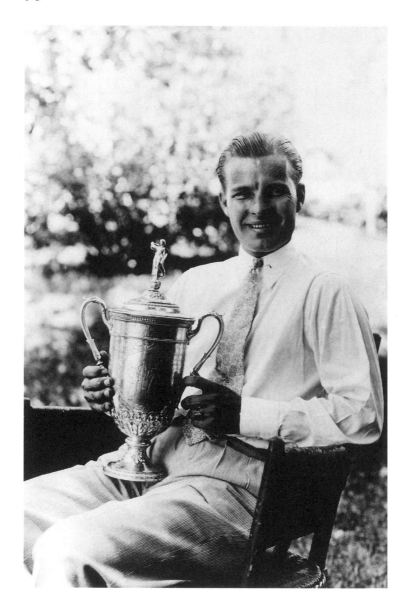

Johnny Goodman with the U. S. Open trophy

CHAPTER V

Walker Cup Play And Other Tournament Play: 1934-1938

Walker Cup Team Play

In the ten years between 1930, when Bobby Jones retired from tournament golf at the age of 28 following his grand slam, and 1940, when Lawson Little, the great amateur who as a professional won the U.S. Open, Johnny Goodman was regarded as a supreme among amateurs.

With the 1929 victory over Jones, Goodman became a thorn in the side of the United States Golf Association. He had finished low amateur in the 1929 U.S. Open next to the winner, Bobby Jones. He was low amateur in the 1932 U.S. Open and went to the finals of the 1932 National Amateur losing, two and one, but not before upsetting Francis Ouimet and beating Seaver and McCarthy, all three having been elected for the 1932 Walker Cup Team.

He acquired the title of "Golf's Forgotten Man" when he was not selected for the American Walker Cup Team in 1932. Something of a storm was raised by this omission, and the question of social discrimination against the player was for the first time brought into the open. Johnny certainly couldn't have been considered a "blue blood", if social status was one of the requirements for membership on the Walker Cup Team at that time.

From the point of view of some individuals, Johnny had not been properly humble in his relations with the USGA at the 1929 National Amateur at Pebble Beach. At that time, Johnny made his living then as a clerk in a sporting goods store. The USGA officials felt that, in some way or other, this cast doubt on his amateur standing. It was tactfully suggested that he might withdraw, but Johnny refused. After that time, he earned his living by selling insurance.

When Goodman went on to win the 1933 U.S. Open, he could no longer be passed by and was chosen for the 1934, 1936, and 1938 Walker Cup Teams and performed admirably. He may go down in history as the only player who had to win the U.S. Open to get on the Walker Cup Team. He played on three Walker Cup Teams, number one on the team both in 1936 and 1938. It is important to remember that both foursome and singles in these years were all contested at 36 holes.

In 1934 and 1936 he won all of his Walker Cup matches. In 1934 at St. Andrews, Scotland, he won both foursome points with Lawson Little and singles point from Honorable Michael Scott. In 1936 at Pine Valley Golf Club, he won both foursome points with Albert "Scotty" Campbell and singles point from Hector Thomson.

In 1938 at St. Andrews, Scotland, he lost both foursome points with Marvin "Bud" Ward, and lost to Hector Thomson.

Total Walker Cup points:

Foursomes: won two and lost one.

Singles: won two and lost one.

In the singles, Goodman defeated the Honorable Michael Scott, the 1933 British Amateur champion, and at age 55 the oldest player to have ever won this tournament.

Hector Thomson was the current British Amateur champion when Goodman defeated him in the Walker Cup matches of 1936 at Pine Valley, New Jersey. Pine Valley was the only match in Walker Cup history where the British did not gain a point. The major factor here, however, was the style of the golf course. Pine Valley, one of America's great courses, had large bunkers guarding most of the entries to its greens. This was in contrast to St. Andrews, in Scotland, which was flat and open which allowed players to employ "bump and run" shots around the greens. Consequently, the British were inexpert with the pitching wedge.

In 1938, the British won the Walker Cup at St. Andrews. This was remarkable in view of the fact they lost the cup to the United States in the nine previous consecutive matches.

The Masters and The National Amateur

The winters in Nebraska are long and cold, prohibiting many opportunities for golf. The Masters comes in early spring giving little preparation time to a golfer living in the far north. The alternative for someone like Goodman, living in the winters of Omaha, Nebraska, was to visit a warmer climate prior to the Masters. Goodman not only couldn't afford the expense of such preparations, he could hardly afford to pay his way from Nebraska to Augusta, Georgia, the site of the Masters. Be reminded that Goodman's competitive golf career coincided with the depth of the nation's greatest depression. On top of the already difficult economic times, Goodman had to pay all of his own expenses in order to retain his status as an amateur within the rules of the USGA. Because of this he

94

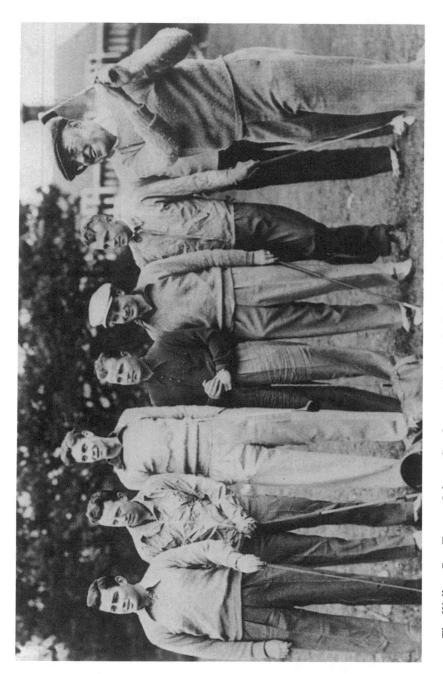

The Walker Cup Team - Johnny Goodman, 4th from the left. Francis Ouimet, Team Captain, is teeing off.

was able to accept only one invitation out of many to play in the Masters Golf Tournament.

In 1935 the Masters Tournament in Augusta, Georgia, established the rule that all previous National Amateur, National Open, and Walker Cup Team members would be invited to play. Johnny Goodman qualified in all three categories and, although invited every year, he could afford to play in only one Masters Tournament and that was in 1936. He shot a 75 in the fourth round and finished in 43rd place.

In the 1935 National Amateur at The Country Club in Cleveland, the 36-hole, semifinal match was held on September 13 and Goodman was defeated by Lawson Little, the eventual winner, who became a great golfer in his own right. Bill Richardson, golf writer of the New York Times, declared the match was the most exciting duel in the 39-year history of the National Amateur. Lawson Little threw four birdies at Goodman in the last six holes. Little went on to become the winner of the U.S. Open as a professional in 1940.

Also in 1935 Johnny Goodman teamed up with Sam Snead at the Greenbrier in West Virginia in an exhibition match against Lawson Little, back to back National Amateur and British Amateur Champion, and Billy Burke, 1931 U. S. Open Champion. Goodman and Snead won the match three and two.

Through being fellow members of the Walker Cup Team and by playing championship golf together, Goodman and Little became close personal friends. When Lawson Little married, Johnny Goodman was his best man.

The following year, 1936, Goodman went to the semifinals in the National Amateur again and was defeated by the eventual winner, Johnny Fisher. In 1937 Goodman was low amateur in the U.S. Open and finally won the U.S. Amateur at last that same year.

Johnny Goodman remained an amateur throughout his tournament career, primarily, because he continued to emulate his boyhood hero, Bobby Jones.

An interview with Willie Tunesa highlights some interesting points about Johnny Goodman. Willie was twice winner of the National Amateur and winner of the British Amateur, as well as three time member and Captain of the Walker Cup Team.

AUTHOR - WHAT WAS YOUR EXPERIENCE AND KNOWLEDGE OF JOHNNY GOODMAN?

Although I never played a match against him, I know he was highly thought of in the world of golf. He wasn't just a flash in the pan so to speak. He was a very steady player and well thought of by his fellow players. For an amateur to win the U. S. Open as he did is a marvelous accomplishment and a great historical event in the history of golf.

I had an opportunity to interview some of the former Walker Cup Team members who were on the team with Johnny Goodman in 1938 when they played the British at St. Andrews. At this time Goodman was considered the premier amateur golfer in the United States. As an example of his status in the world of golf Johnny's picture graced the cover of Time magazine for its June 6, 1938 issue entitled the "King of Swing".

Another of the Walker Cup Team members was Charles Kocsis who is a young 83 years old and still an active amateur golfer currently living in Rochester Hills, Michigan. Charlie was a member of the prestigious Walker Cup Team in 1938, 1949, and 1957.

WHAT KIND OF GUY WAS JOHNNY GOODMAN?

I remember him as a very pleasant kind of guy - rather quiet. He conducted himself as a gentleman, and was a real credit to the game.

HOW WOULD YOU RATE HIS GOLF?
He was a good solid player. Very accurate off the tee and he had a great short game.

DID HE EVER BEAT YOU ON THE COURSE?
Yes, I think he beat me 2 and 1 in one of the National Amateurs we played. I remember I beat him; once too in a match.

WHAT WAS IT LIKE BEING AN AMATEUR IN THOSE DAYS?
It was tough, because to remain an amateur you had to pay all your own expenses - that wasn't easy in the depths of the depression unless you were independently wealthy. To give you an example of how tight the USGA was about amateur status, I was in Mexico in 1948 when I bumped into some friends of mine there. After a lot of conversation, they convinced me to play in the Mexican Amateur that was being held just then. I hadn't planned to play, but I did decide to enter.
Later, Joe Dey, Executive Director of the USGA, wrote to me, questioning whether or not anyone had paid my expenses to play in the tournament. Well, to satisfy him, I had to furnish canceled checks for everything before he was satisfied. I made it clear to him that I always paid all my own expenses when I played in tournaments.

DO YOU STILL PLAY GOLF?
I sure do - played three times last week and shot one round in 74 - plan to keep on playing regardless of the weather here in Michigan.
I wish I could tell you more about Goodman, but let me say again he was a fine person, a credit to the game, and a great player.

Another 1938 Walker Cup Team member that I interviewed was Freddy Haas, Jr., now 80 years old and living in a suburb of New Orleans, Louisiana. Freddie was an amateur in 1945 when he won the Memphis Open. By winning the tournament, he broke Byron Nelson's streak of eleven straight tournament wins. Haas posted an eighteen-under 270 to become the first amateur to capture an important circuit tournament since 1936. Nelson's 276 was good enough to tie for fourth. Freddy turned professional the next year, but this win was one of the highlights of his career.

WHAT WAS YOUR IMPRESSION OF JOHNNY GOODMAN AS A GOLFER IN 1938, WHEN HE PLAYED ON THE WALKER CUP TEAM WITH YOU IN ST. ANDREWS?

Well, actually we kind of held Goodman in awe. He was a real celebrity then, and he was surrounded by people who wanted to be with him. Of course we were with him in practice rounds and all.

WHAT IMPRESSIONS DID YOU HAVE OF HIS GAME?

He undoubtedly was a magnificent player. He was extremely accurate off the tee - not long by today's standards. It was easy to see why he would play well on U. S. Open and National Amateur type courses with their tight fairways and deep rough. His drives were like rifle shots they were so accurate. He was also great around the greens.

WHAT SORT OF GOLF SWING DID JOHNNY HAVE?

He had a short compact swing with little room for error. This gave him the marvelous accuracy he had in his shots.

WHAT ABOUT HIS TEMPERAMENT?

You know, although the competition is usually plentiful

in golf tournaments, very few golfers have the mental toughness and confidence to contend for the major events. Johnny Goodman had these characteristics. He had a great ability to focus and concentrate while playing - didn't have much time for small talk. He was very friendly and outgoing with his teammates and modest despite his achievements.

DID HE PLAY A LOT OF TOURNAMENT GOLF?

Actually, he didn't play very much tournament golf at all. In those days, to remain an amateur in the face of the deep depression was difficult, especially for someone like Goodman who had very limited income.

WHAT PART DID YOU THINK GOODMAN'S CAREER PLAYED IN PROMOTING GOLF?

Johnny Goodman played a great part in promoting golf, especially in view of his background coming from a poor family and having to struggle the way he did. He was a great role model for the young golfers of the day. His desire to remain an amateur and not capitalize on his fame by turning professional had a very positive effect on the world of amateur golf.

I'm glad I had the experience of knowing him and playing golf with him. He was a real credit to the game.

100

1936 Cartoon depicting Johnny Goodman
September 14, 1936
The logical successor to Lawson Little starts his drive for the U.S.
Amateur at Garden City, Long Island, New York

1937

Again, let's look at history that year.

• United States Open Golf
Tournament won by Ralph Guldahl.

• Insulin first used to control diabetes.

• Wall Street Market declines and
signals further serious economic
recession in the United States.

• United States Supreme Court rules
in favor of minimum wage law for women.

• Popular songs, "It's Nice Work If
You Can Get It" and "I've Got My
Love To Keep Me Warm."

• Hitler becomes dictator and head
of Nazi party. Becomes a world threat.

Johnny Goodman - 1937 National Amateur Champion

CHAPTER VI

Winning The 1937
National Amateur [1]

Played on the beautiful Alderwood Country Club on the
banks of the Columbia River in Oregon, this was the first
National Amateur since 1933 where there were 36 holes of
qualifying competition conducted at the championship site to
determine the 64 who would continue in the match play. Roger
Kelley, a 21-year-old law student of Beverly Hills, California,
led the pre-qualifiers with a two under par 142 for 36 holes.

Johnny Goodman got through the pre-qualifying
handily. He was joined by a strong field of favorites to
win - Ray Billows, Frank Strafaci, Chick Evans, Johnny
Fischer, Willie Tunnesa, and C. Ross Somerville, the
former National Amateur champion from Canada.

Many of the greens were impossible to hold with
any sort of pitch shot. A heavy downpour of rain curtailed
the practice round and softened the greens. That proved a
boon to the players the next day. As play progressed,
interest rapidly began to focus upon Goodman, Billows,
Ward, Fischer, Don Moe, and the 47-year-old returnee,
Chick Evans.

Then, in the 36-hole semifinals, Johnny Goodman
and Marvin Ward put on one of the most exciting matches

---

[1] *The Havemeyer trophy awarded to the National Amateur
Champion is the oldest American Championship. It was first
played over 100 years ago in 1895.*

that has ever been staged in a national championship. Finishing the morning round with a two under par 69, Goodman found himself only two up on the handsome Ward, who had built up much more of a reputation for himself at medal play than at match play. Ward's bid had not ended here. Starting the afternoon session with an astonishing burst of sub-par golf, he quickly erased Goodman's lead and actually went ahead on the 24th. From there on the battle raged fiercely, Goodman going ahead on the 32nd and maintaining his margin, as Ward barely missed a nine-footer on the final green to lose the match to Goodman.

Goodman and Billows reached the 36 hole finals. Few final matches in championship history have carried the thrills of this one between Goodman, who had been struggling in vain for the title for many years, and Billows, the latest star in the golfing world. There was a gallery of about 9,000, huge for those days. The Nebraskan simply was too steady for Billows, who was twice winner of the New York State crown. Goodman wore down the erstwhile "Cinderella man" of golf by the painful process of pouring pars at him.

Goodman quit the field of battle two up when they finished the first 18 holes on the bright sunny morning and relentlessly increased his lead as the match wore on. There were only two occasions that afternoon when Billows looked as if he might stage a rally and prevent his determined opponent from reaching his goal.

One of these was on the first hole after the noonday intermission. On that one hole Billows provided a thrill that comes once in lifetime for a gallery. He almost holed out a full wood shot for a double eagle which, had it gone in, would undoubtedly have generated as much excitement in the gallery as Gene Sarazen's two on the par five No.15 at Augusta National in the spring of 1936 did. Billows' tee shot, played with a slight hook (he was pulling many of his drives), stopped in the short rough just off the fairway, and after Goodman belted the ball into the rough up near the green, the New Yorker banged away at a brassie with all his might. The ball set out straight as an arrow, landed short of the green, and stopped not more than eight inches from the pin. He had covered 501 yards with those two blows. The shot put Billows right back into the match, for it left him only one down.

The score didn't remain that way for long, however, for a strong iron shot on the next hole carried Billows' ball over the green, and he was right back where he started, two down with 16 holes to play.

There were two stymies in the morning's play, one against each finalist. The first came on the third hole, a short pitch affair of 125 yards. This one was laid against the Nebraskan, but he proved he could overcome the situation by lofting his ball over Billows' and into the hole after one bounce, for a half. Ray's ball was about six inches from the cup and Johnny's approximately 18 inches behind it. Using a niblick, Goodman pitched his ball over and it went in.

The other stymie on the first 18 came on the 13th hole. This time the nearer ball, Goodman's, was about eight inches from the hole and Billows' approximately two feet behind Johnny's. Billows attempted to loft over, but his ball hit the other and failed to go in the hole.

Of all the words that have been a part of golfing vocabulary, only the word stymie has been incorporated into everyday English. Its meaning carries the original terse definition. When one says he or she is stymied, one is directly blocked from a goal by an unwanted object.

After he captured the 23rd hole in the afternoon round, it seemed as if the New Yorker was on his way.

There, Goodman, catching a bunker on his approach shot, tried to chip out and half-missed, leaving himself a putt too long to hole. Ray was back to only one down, and there was still ample time left for him to rally and gain the honors for which he was a candidate twice before. This, however, was the closest he had ever gotten.

If there was any one hole that proved the turning point in the match, it was the 24th - the dog leg No. 6 - which is 559 yards long. Ray had the misfortune to have to play his second shot from out of a divot, which added to the already intense pressure he must have felt.

By no means was his task made easier when Goodman's pitch, perfectly hit, landed short and ran to within six feet of the hole. Billows was unable to get his ball into the air, and it skidded over the green. He took two to get down and lost the hole, four to five, when Johnny sent his bold putt into the back of the cup.

The bad break seemed to depress Ray's morale, and it was evidenced on the next hole which Johnny won four to five after missing the green with his approach shot. Chipping on, Goodman sank a four-foot putt for his par, while Billows, only 20 feet from the hole in two, took three putts, missing one of three feet for a half.

They halved the 26th, then Billows had to hole a ten-foot putt to hold Goodman even on the 27th, where Ray was off the green from the tee, whereas Goodman was on 12 feet from a birdie two.

With only eight holes left to play, Goodman was four up, and it looked as if the end might come at any time. But with the end in sight, his own lapses and Ray's never-say-die spirit brought the match to the last hole on the course.

When the Nebraskan won the 28th, four to five, as Billows, usually one of the most reliable putters in the game, again set himself a stymie, or at least a partial one, it looked to everyone as if Goodman's constant battering at par had had its paralyzing effect on the Poughkepsie golfer's game. None of the Goodman gallery was much concerned even when Johnny took a bad five on the short 29th, where he pitched into the gully and finally conceded Ray his par three.

He was still leading by three holes and the holes were running out fast. Through carelessness or over confidence Johnny almost lost the next hole, saving it only by pitching 75 yards from the rough to within six inches of the flagstick.

Two more halved holes, and it still was three up for Goodman. On the 32nd, his ball caromed off Billows' into the hole and, on the succeeding one, he had to knock in a ten-foot putt to get a half.

Then came two holes that Goodman probably will always remember, holes that might have cost him the crown he had so eagerly worked for and so long been denied. On the 33rd, the Nebraskan's failure to drop a seven-foot putt gave Ray a chance to hole one of less than a foot for a birdie four.

This reduced Johnny's lead to two holes, and on the next one, the short 207-yard No. 16 (the 34th hole in the match), Goodman saw another hole vanish when he left his ball between six and eight feet from the cup and missed his par. Then it was only one up and two to play - a far different story from what it had been a few holes back.

Both played the 35th hole in par fours, Billows on the green 30 feet from the cup and Goodman 40 feet and having to hole a three foot putt which just got in the hole, the ball being held back by a blade of grass for part of a second that must have seemed to be hours to Goodman.

With a courage seldom demonstrated on the links, Billows overcame his huge deficit, and as he and the Nebraskan stood on the last tee, Johnny was dormie one; Billows had to win the final hole to tie the match.

If Goodman was at all disturbed by the suddenness with which fate had turned her favor from him to the wavy-haired Billows, he didn't show it in his play at the final hole. With two bigshots on the 561-yard hole, he was just short of the green, within easy pitching distance.

These shots put the issue up to Ray, for the Easterner now had to go all out, which is what he did. However, his wood shot had a slight "fade" on it, and his ball wandered to the right, finally stopping in the rough and leaving him with a hanging lie to play to the flagstick, which was placed near his side of the green. It was a difficult shot with not much green to work with.

Once again, Goodman's steadiness in the pinches counted in his favor. With his title perhaps hanging on his next shot, Johnny pitched his ball within six feet of the flagstick - a superb shot under any circumstances, but a truly great one at this nerve-wracking state of the struggle between the two.

Billows, apparently realizing that his magnificent uphill fight had been waged in vain, walked up to his ball, took out his niblick, and pitched his ball to the green, but as it landed, it skidded and ran about nine feet past the flagstick.

Everything now depended on whether or not he could hole the next putt for a birdie and tie the match, but when the ball grazed the side of the cup, Ray walked over and shook hands with the young man from Omaha.

Johnny Goodman mowed down the field with unbreakable calm in winning this tournament. To the select list of immortals who have won both the American Amateur and Open championships another name, Johnny Goodman, was added at the Alderwood Country Club. As Johnny Goodman, Omaha insurance agent, annexed the 41st National Amateur crown, he joined four other distinguished linksmen who previously won both titles - Jerry Travers, Francis Ouimet, Charles (Chick) Evans, and Bobby Jones.

Goodman, who first gained national renown when he eliminated Jones in the first round of the Amateur Championship in 1929, the only other time that the event had been staged in the Golden West, attained his life's ambition when he defeated the slender 23 year-old Ray Billows, member of the Dutchess Club in Poughkepsie, New York, where he was in the employ of a printing establishment.

Armed with a refreshing drink in the clubhouse of the Alderwood Country Club immediately after his two-up victory over Ray Billows, Johnny Goodman, new amateur golf champion, declared that he was never worried during the last crucial holes of match.

"If I win, I win; if I lose, I lose," he said. "That's all there is to it." He was disgusted with himself for missing a short putt on the 15th green in the afternoon, he added.

"I've achieved my three ambitions," he told golf officials who gathered around the new champion as they discovered him alone with a reporter in the clubhouse. "I wanted to play on the Walker Cup Team, win the National Open, and the National Amateur, and now I've done them all."

At the trophy presentation Johnny made a brief speech where he said: "I'm sorry Ray there aren't two titles to be awarded - the final match was the toughest of my career." He went on to say: "This is the happiest moment of my life."

"What are you going to do now, turn pro?" he was asked. "No," was his decisive answer, and he didn't expand on it, except to say again, "I love the game too much to make it a business".

It's interesting to note that the newspaper in Portland, Oregon, *The Oregonian* included Johnny Goodman's winning of the 1937 National Amateur on a list of the seven most important stories of 1937.

Today, with Goodman's achievements in golf, winning the 1933 National United States Open against the professionals and the 1937 National Amateur, turning professional would have gained him substantial financial rewards. An insight into the value of golf to Johnny Goodman and the importance to him of remaining an amateur was demonstrated in 1933 when he won the United States Open. At that time he was deluged with offers to turn professional. One would have to admit that the commercial temptations were not as great then as they are now. With the meager prize money then, one had to have a good club pro job in hand to even consider the tour as it was then. His opportunity to turn professional was greatest after winning the United States Open. Even then, most knowledgeable people felt winning the Open could be worth at least $50,000, which was, to say the least, a lot of money during the depth of the Depression.

By winning the Amateur in 1937 Goodman became the first golfer since Jones to win both the U.S. Open and National Amateurs. As a sidelight, the only department in which Goodman exceeded Jones was that he made six holes-in-one in his lifetime, while Jones had made only two.

Goodman demonstrated strong character through his determination to succeed and overcome the obstacles he faced. He was a very self-effacing champion and he had achieved his final ambition - winning the National Amateur Golf Tournament. He was chasing a dream, and that dream came true.

Johnny Goodman with the U. S. Amateur trophy, 1937

*Parade in Omaha following Johnny Goodman's
1937 National Amateur Victory*

*The marriage of Josephine and Johnny Goodman,
June 1938*

CHAPTER VII

The Closing Years
Of His Life

In the year 1938 Johnny Goodman was still selling insurance, making a reasonable living, and was a celebrated member of the Omaha Field Club where he started as a caddie. He still lived in a furnished room in Omaha with a very fine family named Reeves, and spent a lot of his free time playing pinochle with his bothers and some of his friends. He also enjoyed playing bridge. Roman Catholic, Johnny's most constant golfing companion was Father John Palvbicki, pastor of his church.

He still dated the girl he first met in 1929, a pretty stenographer Josephine Kersigo, and they were married later in 1938, the year that he again played the number one position on the Walker Cup Team. His play that year was less than he wanted it to be. In June, 1938, his golf skills were so recognized in the world of golf that his picture appeared on the cover of *Time* magazine.

In 1939 and 1940 the nation was still in the depths of an economic depression. Goodman, just married in 1938 and unable to earn money playing golf as an amateur, had to concentrate on making a living to support his new family. He was only able to play in a very limited number of state and local tournaments. The 1940 Walker Cup matches were canceled because Great Britain was in a struggle for its very life in a war with Nazi Germany. The matches weren't resumed until after World War II, in 1947.

Just prior to World War II, Johnny qualified for and played in the 1941 National Amateur at his home club, the Omaha Field Club, in Omaha, Nebraska. He lost his first round match in extra holes. He said later that was one of his greatest disappointments. Our nation declared war on the Axis nations, Germany, Italy, and Japan, in December of that same year after the infamous Japanese attack on Pearl Harbor.

Johnny was inducted into the service during the war, took his basic training as a private at Camp Lee, Virginia, and then served overseas in India. While serving in India, he received another invitation to play in the 1942 Masters Golf Tournament in Augusta, Georgia. From 1935 on, Johnny had received invitations to play in the Masters on the strength of his winning both the National Open and the National Amateur. The address on the envelope that he received while in India was marked out and crossed out over and over, but had been forwarded to the other side of the world until it reached its army post office destination. Enclosed was the formal invitation and a small card from Clifford Roberts, Chairman of the Augusta National, announcing the Masters for 1942 had been canceled "due to world conditions." Johnny, needless to say, was thrilled to continue to be honored by the Masters invitations.

The tendency when writing about someone of great accomplishments is to idolize that person - to avoid anything that may be disreputable or negative in his character. Of course, doing so would be unrealistic. He was human and had faults like the rest of us. A French philosopher of the 16th century made a statement that contains a real truth: "There is no man so good, who, were he to submit all his thoughts and actions to the scrutiny of the law, would not deserve hanging at least ten times during his lifetime."

In gathering material for this story, many of the

people with whom I talked were reluctant to criticize Johnny. Yet, I did have the impression that at times he was too easily persuaded to engage in activities in his business and social life that were not in his best interests. Some of the people around him were apparently attempting to capitalize personally on his fame.

After the war, Johnny worked for his brother-in-law managing a social club called The Birchwood in Omaha. Injuries and illness beset him after his return from overseas in India. At one point, he was critically injured in an auto accident with a severely broken left arm. Although he was only 38 years old at the time of this accident it greatly diminished his ability to play at the level of his peak years. After the accident he no longer played competitive golf to any extent, but maintained a strong interest in golf to the end of his life. Johnny's son remembered that one of his father's greatest regrets was that he wished he had played in more golf tournaments when he was younger.

In 1950, when their son John was only three years old, Josephine persuaded Johnny to move to California for she was weary of the long winters of Omaha. Johnny was successful as a sales representative for the Canada Dry Bottling Company in California, but when the company began a down-sizing program, he retired.

The Goodmans lived in Southgate, a suburb of Los Angeles, California. His son John, a virtual look-alike for his dad, recalls that his dad was very easygoing and never tried to pressure him toward a career in golf. His son's interests as a teenager growing up were in other sports. His son said that most every Sunday after church he, his dad, and his mother would play golf together in the afternoons at the Southgate Course. He remembers his dad as having a good sense of humor and a great deal of patience with people, a characteristic that made him a good teacher. He remembers, too, that his dad was meticulous in the way he dressed, and especially in the way he cared for his golf equipment. John expressed genuine respect for his father, and it was clear that he was close to him, and remembered his years growing up with his father as happy ones.

Josephine expressed no regrets about the past and was reluctant to dwell on it. Yet, she did comment that when Johnny was a young successful golfer and an orphan, he had no parents or mentor to guide him. She said, "Can you imagine the heights he could have reached if he had a father like the father of the young Tiger Woods?" One can only imagine.

Josephine said that Johnny always thought of himself as an amateur, yet, because of his love of golf he did teach golf in his later years at the Big Tee Golf Center in Buena Park, California. He was not a professional in the sense that he held such a position at a club. What was really important to her was that Johnny will be remembered by all who touched his life as being a good sportsman and gentleman on the links, as well as being generous and kind in every way. He was a gentleman - a term, unfortunately, not much in use these days - a courteous and decent man. Making lots of money was not a goal in his life, as evidenced by the fact that he remained an amateur when the temptations to turn professional were great.

In his later years, Johnny Goodman said "I've enjoyed my life, I accomplished what I wanted to do in golf, made good friends, was happy with my family, was sustained by a deep faith in God, and enjoyed my work. What more can a person ask for?"

Josephine said, "He had a successful career and, foremost, was a good husband and father." Most of us would be happy to end our lives with that kind of testimonial.

An insight into Johnny's temperament was related to me by his nephew Jack Atkins of Omaha: "I played what was to be his last round of golf with him, two weeks before he died." To illustrate his determination, Jack related: "On the second hole his drive struck an embankment and rolled down a steep hill." I told him: "Hit another, we're just playing for fun" He said "I don't do such things". He pulled out a five wood, climbed down the ravine, didn't even take relief from the cart path, and hit his second shot 220 yards straight down the middle and parred the hole. His competitive spirit was an ongoing mind set that carried through to the end of his life".

At the age of 22, Johnny's son John was an active reservist in the Marine Corps when he learned that his father had suddenly, without warning, suffered a heart attack. By the time John got home, his father had died, on August 8, 1970. He was only 61 years of age. Johnny's body was brought home to Omaha with an honored burial in a plot owned by the mother of his wife, Josephine, at St. John's cemetery in Omaha, where Josephine plans to be buried. His nephew Jack was one of the pallbearers at the funeral.

Johnny Goodman was a waif who survived personal adversity and turned it into opportunity. He died pretty much in relative obscurity, as many other persons of great achievement have throughout history. Johnny Goodman's achievements in the game of golf were many and significant. He defeated the great Bobby Jones, won the world's two major golf championships of his time - the United States Open and the United States National Amateur, competed in the prestigious international Walker Cup matches, and became a golf legend.

Johnny Goodman was enshrined in Nebraska's sports Hall of Fame at the Hillcrest Country Club in Lincoln, Nebraska, on May 8, 1990. His wife, Josephine, and son, John, were brought to Nebraska for the occasion - a wonderful banquet where he and his record were honored. David Fay, the Executive Director of the United States Golf Association attended, along with many of Nebraska's dignitaries. Fay stated in his address, "Many people always ask me at every Open, 'Who was the last amateur to win the Open?' and, of course, the answer is Johnny Goodman." Johnny's wife Josephine commented on how proud Johnny would have been of this special occasion.

While his son, John, was in town for the Hall of Fame celebration he and his son - Johnny Goodman's grandson - visited the University of Nebraska in Lincoln where Johnny had won a golf scholarship from the newspaper, *The World-Herald*, when he graduated from high school. Johnny's grandson decided then to attend the same university and is now in his senior year.

I had the pleasure of talking with Johnny Goodman's widow, Josephine, who is now 86 years old and living in Anaheim, California. Their only child, John R. Goodman, lives in nearby Lake Forest, California. He is now 49 and a longtime member of the police force in Westminister, California. I had an interesting conversation with him, as well as with one of Johnny's nephews, John R. Atkins, Jr., of Omaha, Nebraska, who knew Johnny well. All of these people, along with a boyhood friend of Johnny's, a retired professional golfer in Omaha, Matt Zadalis, were most helpful in completing the story of Johnny's life.

Johnny Goodman and Josephine

Johnny giving Josephine a few pointers

CHAPTER VIII

Reminiscing With Josephine

Josephine is a young 86 years old with a delightful and charming personality. She is an attractive woman with a bright enthusiastic manner. She spoke lovingly of her husband Johnny as she recalled the past. She wasted no time in convincing me that, although 26 years had passed since Johnny's death, the many memories she has of his life were still very clear in her mind.

She showed me a scrap book of newspaper clippings and pictures that she had kept over the years. It was so big I could hardly lift it! Dating back almost 70 years, the pages were beginning to crumble. My meeting with Josephine gave me an excellent insight into the personality of Johnny Goodman. It goes without saying, wives know their husbands' best of all.

As Josephine began to reminisce about Johnny it quickly became apparent that she loved him dearly. She said, "He was a real handsome guy, blonde hair and deep blue eyes." She went on to say, "You know at my age I realize life is made up of good and bad memories. The good memories seem to stand out and the bad ones seem to fade, so I'll perhaps remember the good memories first."

*AUTHOR - IF THERE ARE ANY QUESTIONS YOU
DON'T CARE TO ANSWER, JUST SAY SO, I'LL
UNDERSTAND.*

Oh! No, I don't think we'll have any problem there.
I would like to know, though, why you are taking the time and
effort to write about Johnny and his career when it all happened
so long ago. I think he has been pretty well forgotten. Why,
just this past June when they were writing about past winners
of the U. S. Open in the Orange County newspaper, they
completely left Johnny's name out.

*THAT'S THE REASON I WANT TO WRITE THIS
RECORD, SO THAT HE WON'T BE FORGOTTEN. I
BELIEVE HE WAS ONE OF THIS NATION'S GREAT
AMATEUR GOLFERS. I'VE ALWAYS THOUGHT HIS
LIFE STORY FASCINATING.*

WHEN DID YOU FIRST GET TO KNOW JOHNNY?

That was way back in grade school in Omaha,
Nebraska. I was only about six years old. Johnny was
only about six months older than I was. I can remember he
won a golf tournament when he was in high school. We
didn't start really dating until we were both out of high
school.

*DO YOU REMEMBER MUCH ABOUT THOSE EARLY
YEARS?*

Not really. I know Johnny was from a big family
and although he never talked much about his family, he did
love his mother dearly. When he was real little and just
starting to caddie he would skip church on Sunday mornings
and go to the Field Club golf course in Omaha to caddie.
He would get there ahead of the other kids that were in
church. He said sometimes he would caddie double. As

soon as he was through he'd hurry home and give his mother the money he earned. It was in those years the family was big and without a father, and they desperately needed money to stay alive.

DID HE EVER TALK MUCH ABOUT HIS DIFFICULT CHILDHOOD YEARS?

No, he didn't. You see, we were both from poor families and having a rough time. We had a lot in common. There were five in my family and my mother was a widow. After my father died - he had worked in a coal mine in Pennsylvania - we moved to Omaha. Mother was determined that her sons would not have to work in the coal mines and that's why we moved. As you know, in those days working in a coal mine was a horrible experience and my father died from black lung - a very common illness then. My mother's life is another story, but she was a very courageous woman in the way she managed our family as a widow and did so well. When she came to Omaha she wasn't even able to speak English.

I think Johnny didn't talk about his childhood because he didn't want people to know he was so poor. He always had a grateful attitude about almost everything. I suppose that attitude grew out of his childhood when he had so little.

DID HE TALK ABOUT HIS EXPERIENCES AT THE UNIVERSITY OF NEBRASKA?

No, he said he liked the school, but he really wanted to play golf more than anything else. I'm sure he would be proud to know that his grandson is now a senior at the University of Nebraska. He is majoring in criminology, and is not into golf at all.

WHAT DID JOHNNY DO AFTER LEAVING THE
UNIVERSITY?

He lived with the Webster family in Omaha when he came back. The family were friends of his. To earn money Johnny sold insurance for the Mutual of Omaha. He wasn't especially successful at that, but it gave him a chance to save some money and play in tournaments. You know, in those days golf was a rich man's game. He was very careful about retaining his amateur status and not receiving money for playing golf. I was working as a policy-writer for the same company. It's hard to believe now but I was making $15.00 a week and glad to have a job.

DID YOU EVER WATCH HIM PLAY IN ANY GOLF
TOURNAMENTS?

Yes, I was in the gallery when he won the United States Open in 1933 in Chicago. I took some vacation to see him play. I had a sister living in the area and was able to stay with her. I think Johnny stayed with some friends near the course. It was hot as blazes that week. I followed him for all of his matches. I was so excited when Johnny won by just one shot. He was one happy guy that day.

YOUR SON JOHN TOLD ME HIS DAD WAS
VERY METICULOUS IN THE CARE OF
HIS GOLF EQUIPMENT. WAS THIS
CHARACTERISTIC OF HIM?

Oh yes! Especially in the way he dressed on or off the golf course. I think he had so little in the way of decent clothes when he was young that he really prided himself in always dressing as well as possible and being meticulous in his appearance and in everything he did.

*WHY DO YOU SUPPOSE JOHNNY NEVER
TURNED PROFESSIONAL?*

His hero then was Bobby Jones, and he wanted to be just like him - just play amateur golf and have a job that would let him do that. He really looked up to Bobby and over the years they became good friends. Of course turning pro in those days didn't mean you'd make lots of money like it does today. You had to get a job as a pro at a club to support yourself. But Johnny always wanted to be an amateur like his idol Bobby Jones.

WHO WAS HIS BEST FRIEND?

The only one outside of his family he was real close to was Lawson Little. They played together on the Walker Cup team in 1934 - paired together and beat the British team. I think it was Cyril Tolley and someone else - beat them badly eight up with six holes to play. Lawson Little beat Johnny in the second round of the 1929 U. S. Amateur at Pebble Beach. He said Johnny was the toughest competitor he had ever played against. They were very close. Johnny was best man at Lawson's wedding in Chicago in February of 1936. I understand in the same year Little turned pro - won the United States Open in 1940 - he was a great golfer like Johnny. He did have a father though, I think he was a Colonel in the Army.

Johnny spent a lot of time with his brothers - he was very close to them. Out of the thirteen children in the family the youngest and I think only one who is living is Tom, who lives in Phoenix, Arizona.

WHEN WERE YOU AND JOHNNY MARRIED?

We were married on June 29, 1938 - we were both 30 years old. We had a small wedding in a Polish church called Saint Stanislaus. Those were rough times with the depression and all. We lived with my mother back then - all her children were grown and gone. My mother had a big house at 3973 H Street in Omaha. Johnny and I both worked to make ends meet.

WAS THE CHURCH A PART OF JOHNNY'S LIFE?

Yes, we were both Roman Catholics, and Johnny and I felt the church was a real part of our lives. It still is an important part of my life. I think his faith supported him throughout his life.

*I UNDERSTAND THAT JOHNNY EVENTUALLY
WENT TO WORK FOR YOUR SISTER'S
HUSBAND MR. ATKINS WHO WAS
A BEER DISTRIBUTOR IN OMAHA.*

Yes. They formed a social club called the Burchwood which Johnny helped manage. It was a very successful club.

WHEN WAS YOUR SON JOHN BORN?

He was born on February 10, 1947. We would have liked to have had more children, but that's just the way it turned out. I'm so grateful for my son.

WHAT KIND OF PARENT WAS JOHNNY?

He loved children and I know he was a good father. Perhaps one of the reasons was that he never really had one.

*WHERE WERE YOU ALL WHEN THE UNITED
STATES ENTERED THE WAR IN DECEMBER 1941?*

We were in Omaha. I'll never forget. Johnny and I were riding in our car that Sunday looking at places near the Omaha Field Club when the news came that Pearl Harbor had been attacked. Johnny's remark was, "Well, there goes your house". You see, we had planned to build a home.

He later went into the service and served in New Delhi, India. He was discharged in 1946. He was really too old to be going into the service - he was 33 when he went in. After he came home he said he never liked the service and that he was glad to get out. When he came back and played he never recovered his game. As a matter of fact, he later had a serious automobile accident - he was traveling on an icy road and tried to avoid hitting an animal - broke his arm very seriously. I don't think he ever fully recovered.

HOW WOULD YOU DESCRIBE HIS CHARACTER AND PERSONALITY?

He had a great sense of humor - never took himself too seriously. He didn't have one face for the public and a different one when he was home - he was always the same. He was generous - after he'd win a tournament, if a friend was admiring the trophy he'd end up giving it to them. We don't have a single trophy that he won - I don't even have the gold medal he received when he won the U. S. Open in 1933. John still has the golf clubs and the putter he used to win the Open - John isn't into golf much now though.

Johnny was good-natured - didn't look on the bad side of things and was able to something good in everything. He had lots of golfing friends and thoroughly enjoyed golf up to the day he died.

As I've said before he was a good father and husband - my life with him was good. He sure was determined when it came to golf. I remember one time in early winter we went out to the Field Club and there was some ice and some scattering of snow on the ground. He got out of the car and went and started to practice. I couldn't believe it - it was too cold for me to even get out of the car. He always worked so damn hard practicing.

WHY AND WHEN DID YOU DECIDE TO MOVE TO CALIFORNIA?

I told Johnny I just didn't want to spend any more long cold winters in Omaha - I wanted to go to southern California. That was in 1950. Johnny agreed. I had a sister who lived in Bell in southern California. He drove down, found an apartment, and found a job with Canada Dry Bottling Company and then we followed. The trip to California is one I really wanted to make. John, who was only three at the time, traveled by train, in the middle of the winter. I'll never forget - we were traveling through western Nebraska and Wyoming and the conductor called us over to the other side of the car and pointed out the hundreds of cattle in the fields frozen to death.

HOW DID HE GET ALONG IN HIS WORK THERE?

He did real well as a salesman and of course it was a help that he was pretty well known. At times he would travel as far as Arizona and he always tried to take us with him. He worked there for a good while and he and his boss got along just great. Then the company, as they say now, did some downsizing and both Johnny and his boss lost their jobs. I think in the eyes of the company they were both too old. There was no retirement plan for them, either.

WHAT DID JOHNNY DO THEN?

Well, he was in his fifties by then. He was reluctant to change his amateur status, but he became a professional when he began teaching golf at the Bellflower Golf Center, a nine-hole par three golf course and driving range near Los Angeles. He loved to work with people and teach. They flocked to him for instruction. He did his best to imbue in others the love he had for golf. He still played golf, but very little competitive golf. He loved golf up to the day he died.

I worked for the Trans American Insurance Company as a stenographer. I don't think insurance companies and banks pay very much money though.

ALL OF THE POSITIVE THINGS YOU ARE SAYING REFLECT YOUR LOVE FOR JOHNNY, BUT LIKE ALL HUMANS HE MUST HAVE HAD SOME FAULTS. WHAT WERE THEY?

I suppose it was his complete love of the game which meant his being away from home a lot to play golf. Yet, his career in golf was pretty much winding down after we were married in 1938. I think too, from a material standpoint, he never really capitalized on being a golf celebrity. Of course the times and the fact that he very much wanted to remain an amateur made it difficult. Living through a depression and a war didn't help. As to his faults, I will say that on balance I will always remember him being a good father and husband.

DID JOHNNY HAVE ANY REGRETS?

He did say he wished he had played in more tournaments when he was younger. Yet when you think about it with the depression in mind, it would have been hard for him to find the money to play more and still keep his amateur standing. You had to pay your own way, you know.

JOHNNY DIED AT AN EARLY AGE. DID HE HAVE ANY WARNING ABOUT AN IMPENDING HEART ATTACK?

No he didn't. As I remember it, he always had good health. We were living in South Gate at the time. One Saturday he said he didn't feel well. We had just gotten back from a trip. It was August 8, 1970. He said, "I think I'll just stay in bed today." Later in the day I heard him gasping for breath, and I went into his room and his face looked so ashen. I knew something was wrong so, I called my sister who was living nearby. Our son John was away on active duty with the Marine Corps. My sister called the rescue squad which came right away. They lifted him from the bed and told me to leave the room and they tried to resuscitate him. After a while they came out and said he was gone. I couldn't stop crying - he was only 60 years old. I appreciated and loved him so much. I still miss him. He was buried in Omaha. That was a sad day for us.

I UNDERSTAND HE WAS LATER INDUCTED INTO THE NEBRASKA GOLF HALL OF FAME IN LINCOLN, NEBRASKA.

Yes, that was on May 8, 1990. It was a very special banquet honoring Johnny. Hundreds of people were there and David Fay, the Executive Director of the USGA was there and talked to the audience about Johnny. I remember he mentioned that at every U. S. Open now they ask, "Who was the last amateur to win the Open?" and of course Johnny's name comes up again. They gave me a beautiful bronze plaque that I had trouble getting through the x-ray machine when we flew back to California. The Hall of Fame paid our airfare, which I thought was nice of them. I was so proud to hear all the good things said about Johnny. I just wish he could have heard it all.

PART II

Observations on Golf Past and Present

CHAPTER IX

Entertaining Anecdotes on Tournament Golf From the Past

W hat follows are some humorous and interesting stories about tournament play in the 1920's and 1930's involving some of golf's great players, including Bobby Jones, Walter Hagen, and Gene Sarazen.

Walter Hagen

The great Walter Hagen didn't win eleven national and five PGA championships on his consummate golfing skills alone. He also relied on cunning gamesmanship of which he was the absolute master.

The crafty Sir Walter toyed with opponents' minds like yo-yos. He tricked his fellow competitors into using the wrong clubs. He ticked them off by taking forever to size up an easy shot. He made them squirm with offhand remarks that shattered their confidence. And he made them stew by deliberately showing up late for his starts.

If his opponents started peeking at his club selections so they could follow his lead, Hagen would con them. He once tricked Al Watrous in the 1925 PGA Championship at Olympia Fields near Chicago. The two were tied as they teed off on the 18th hole, a dangerous par-5 with water fronting the green. Although Hagen hit the longer drive, his ball landed in the rough on the left. Watrous, whose ball lay in the fairway, was away, so he had to play first. He'd planned to use a long iron and lay up short of the water, but then he looked over to Sir Walter, who was taking practice swings with a wood. To Watrous, that meant Hagen had a good lie and was going for the green on his second shot. Figuring that if Hagen was using a wood, so would he. Watrous replaced his iron with a wood - and drilled his shot right into the water. Hagen then smugly put away his wood and pulled out a long iron - the one he had intended to use all along. He played safely to the fairway and went on to par the hole and win the match from a duped Watrous.

The Haig often used a wrinkle on this ploy. He'd play a three-iron but take something off the hit - basically, hitting the three-iron to a five-iron distance. By hiding the "soft" shot in a big swing motion - like a baseball pitcher with a good change-up - Hagen could fool a peeker into going full bore with a three-iron and knocking the ball 20 yards past the green.

Claude Harmon, winner of the 1948 Masters, claimed Hagen sometimes played with mismarked clubs to fool those who dared eavesdrop when the Haig asked for a club from his caddie. "Hagen had a jacked-up set of irons - the four-iron was marked five, and so forth," said Harmon, "and you could get into big trouble" trying to match what club Hagen had requested.

Hagen loved to psych out opponents by strolling over and peering into their bags, then shaking his head and walking away. And on the green, he'd study their putts and then gesture that they were impossible to make.

"Make the hard shots look easy and the easy shots look hard," Sir Walter once said. He drove opponents nuts and threw off their rhythm when, at a crucial time in the match, he'd spend several long minutes studying a "difficult" shot. He once sent to the clubhouse for a folding chair, so that his biggest rival, Gene Sarazen, could sit down while Hagen took his sweet time studying a simple chip shot.

Arriving late to the tee was what Hagen did best.. Many old pros did that to rookies back then - without penalty of disqualification. Only Hagen did it with style.

A lover of wine, women, and song - although not necessarily in that order - Sir Walter often arrived at the golf course still wearing his tuxedo from the night before. He then leisurely changed his shoes, put on his fresh white linen knickers, and strolled to the tee.

A young Byron Nelson fell victim to this ploy at the General Brock Open at Niagra Falls. Nelson, then unknown and unsure of himself, surprised the field by leading after three rounds. On the final day, Nelson, who was to be paired with Hagen, arrived early at the tee, where he fidgeted and fretted and counted the minutes until the his start. Then word came that the Haig would be late. Poor Nelson paced back and forth and took hundreds of practice swings. Two hours later Hagen finally showed up in a white-on-white silk shirt, gold cuff links, and slicked back hair. "Hi, boy," he said to Nelson.

"It's . . . it's a real big honor," stammered the star-struck rookie. His nerves were so frazzled from waiting that he shot a shaky 42 on the front nine, lost his lead, and finished in second place behind Hagen.

Sir Walter's gamesmanship was at its peak during the 1919 U. S. Open at Brae Burn Country Club near Boston. Hagen and Mike Brady had tied after the final round and were set to meet in a playoff the next day.

On the evening of the playoff, Hagen and entertainer Al Jolson donned high tops and tails and squired several

chorus girls to a wild party that swung until dawn.
Sometime during the night, a well-meaning friend told
Hagen, "For God's sake, Walter, why don't you go to bed
and get some sleep so you'll be in shape for the playoff
tomorrow. You can be sure Mike has been in bed and been
sleeping for hours." Hagen laughed and said, "He may be
in bed, right enough, but he ain't sleeping any more than I
am."

The only sleep Hagen caught was a catnap while
being driven to the course where, still decked out in white
tie and tails, he arrived late as usual. While officials gave
Hagen time to change into his clothes, a frustrated Brady
cooled his heels and learned about Hagen's cocky remark
from the previous night.

So he tried to give Hagen a dose of his own
medicine. On the first tee, Brady made a big production
of rolling up his sleeves and spitting on his hands before
teeing off. But Hagen got even. On the second hole, he
sidled up to Brady and whispered, "Mike, you oughta roll
those sleeves back down. You're letting everyone see
how the muscles in your forearms are quivering. It's a
dead giveaway." Brady then hit his tee shot into the woods
bordering the fairway and wound up with a double-bogey
six. Hagen won the championship by a stroke.

Letter-Perfect Scam
1922-Walter Hagen and Gene Sarazen

Before a big match between Walter Hagen and Gene
Sarazen at the Westchester-Biltmore in 1922, Sarazen
received an Orange tie enclosed with a fan letter from a
Ziegfeld show girl who said she desperately wanted him
to beat the Haig.

"Don't look for me in the gallery," said the note.

"I don't want you to take your mind off Hagen. I want you to wear this tie for good luck."

On the day of the match, Sarazen donned the tie, and every chance he got, he scoped the gallery for the show girl. "It was raining and the colors of the tie ran all over my shirt and I was a mess," Sarazen recalled. "Not only that, but I spent a lot of time looking around for that girl and I lost my concentration."

During a break at the turn, Hagen told Sarazen, "Say, that's a handsome tie you've got on. Where'd you get it?"

"A friend," Sarazen replied.

"Is this friend your mysterious admirer, a Follies girl who wanted you to pay strict attention to beating me?"

"Why, yes," Sarazen. "How did you know?" But one look at Hagen's grinning face and Sarazen knew the letter had been written by none other than the Haig himself.

Al Watrous
1932 PGA Championship

Al Watrous felt so sorry for his opponent that he decided to concede him a putt. But before long Watrous felt sorry he ever did it.

He chose to violate an unwritten rule in golf - never give consolation to the enemy. His compassionate decision backfired at the 1932 PGA Championship on the Keller Course in St. Paul, Minnesota, during a 36-hole match against the Scotsman Bobby Cruickshank.

Watrous, winner of 34 tournaments, had built a huge, seemingly insurmountable lead. Nine up with only 13 holes to play on the par-3 sixth hole, the devastated Cruickshank resignedly conceded Watrous's short three-foot putt for par. After surveying his own six-footer that he needed for par, Cruickshank turned to Watrous and lamented, "This is the worst beating I've ever had."

The words seemed to soften Watrous's competitive backbone. Sure, he wanted to win, but he didn't want to humiliate a fellow professional competitor. Recalled Watrous, "I would be going ten up if he missed the putt. Feeling a bit sorry for him and not wanting to see him go down in double figures, I conceded him the putt.

"I can remember so clearly that as we walked off the green to the next tee, we passed a man who had observed the play and the conceded putt. As I went by him, I heard him say to another spectator, 'He shouldn't have done that! He might be sorry for that!'"

Watrous didn't think much of the comment until Cruickshank won the next three holes with a birdie and two pars. "I still remember the change in attitude of both of us as we went to the tenth tee", recalled Watrous, the longtime pro at Oakland Hills Country Club near Detroit. "Earlier we had been discussing Bobby's chances of getting a job (as a golf pro) at one of the Detroit courses and how I could help him. Suddenly, Bobby was all business. The friendliness went out the window. He could sense that he was back in the match."

Watrous played well, but Cruickshank played brilliantly, dazzling the gallery with spectacular putting. On 12 straight holes after the famous conceded putt, Cruickshank had an amazing nine one-putts. One of them was a 70-footer on the 15th hole. Shooting six-under on the back nine, he knocked in another long putt for a birdie at 18 to force a sudden-death playoff.

Watrous tried hard to forget that conceded putt as they halved the first three overtime holes. On the 140-yard par-3 fourth hole, it looked like his nice-guy blunder would not cost him the championship after all. Cruickshank took a bogey four, while Watrous, who placed his tee shot just two feet from the hole, hadn't even made his second stroke.

Cruickshank started to shake hands with Watrous but figured he'd wait until Watrous made the putt. But Watrous's delicate downhill putt skipped past the hole and stopped not more than a foot away. It looked like a simple tap-in. Watrous thought that Cruickshank would graciously concede the putt, but the Scot was not about to do any such thing - not after he'd seen what a tremendous impact that conceded sixth-hole putt had on him. Then, to the gasps of the gallery, Watrous's easy one-foot putt skirted the cup. Unbelievably, Watrous had three-putted from two feet away. Both golfers halved the hole in bogey fours.

On the next hole Watrous was so rattled that he blew a three-foot putt that would have tied Cruickshank, who holed a six-footer for par and an incredible come-from-behind win.

What did Watrous learn from this match? "Don't ever concede your opponent a putt - not even a two-incher!"

Gene Sarazen Fans
1923 PGA Championship

Gene Sarazen won the 1923 PGA Championship thanks to the blatant cheating of his loyal fans.

Sarazen, one of America's greatest golfers, was not aware of this partisan chicanery. But he was certainly aware that the gallery at the Pelham (New York) Country Club desperately wanted him to win. After all, he had grown up in the area, where people knew him under his given name of Eugene Saraceni. They all considered him their local hero.

For this 36-hole match play event, Sarazen, the

defending champion, was pitted against his keenest rival, Walter Hagen, the 1921 winner. Unfortunately for the Haig, he had to contend not only with his gifted opponent, but also with Sarazen's fans, including several of the club's red-sweatered caddies who were loyal to a fault - literally.

The first sign that the fans would help their man win came on the 14th green, which was guarded by a water hazard. Sarazen hit his second shot much too strong. The ball was headed toward the pond when a quick-thinking fan in a red sweater stuck out his foot and stopped the ball from rolling into the water.

"I should have had an easy win [on the 14th hole], but I managed to halve the hole," Hagen said in his autobiography. "After that, I kept my eyes open for the boys in the red sweaters." But he couldn't keep watch over all of them.

Hagen and Sarazen were tied after 36 holes and went to a sudden-death playoff. They halved the 37th and came to the 38th, which was bordered by houses on the left. The gallery uttered a collective moan when Sarazen hooked his drive over a fence. The last he or Hagen heard of the ball it was rattling in between the houses. Officials declared it out of bounds, so Sarazen hit another shot, this time right down the fairway. Recalled Hagen, "With the two stroke penalty he had incurred with his out-of-bounds shot, I figured I could win easily if I played safely down to the right."

Confident that Sarazen could never recover from the penalty, Hagen hit a safe drive to the middle of the fairway and walked jauntily toward his ball. But to his shock, Hagen heard people in the gallery shout that Sarazen's first ball had been found and, even more incredibly, it rested inside the fence!

When Hagen walked over to take a look, he was

flabbergasted. Sarazen's ball was lying neatly on top of the grass a few yards from where kids had made a huge hole in the fence to sneak through onto the golf course. "Witnesses" said the ball had indeed gone out of bounds but it "miraculously" had bounced back through the hole in the fence.

Sarazen had no way of knowing that the ball had been conveniently moved by an "outside agency" - one of his devoted but misguided fans who had tossed it back into play. All Sarazen knew was that by a twist of fate he had been given a reprieve. He didn't have to take a penalty shot after all.

Buoyed by this tremendous break, Sarazen hit a magnificent second shot within a foot of the hole for a certain birdie three. Hagen shook his head in disbelief. Then, obviously shaken by this stunning turn of events, the Haig put his second shot in a trap, short of the green. "Suddenly, an easy victory for me had turned into defeat," he recalled. "There was nothing for me to do except to walk over and congratulate Gene."

And what of Sarazen's out-of-bounds ball that so amazingly bounced back into play? Said the Haig:

"I've never to this day doubted that such luck could happen, but having Gene's ball jump back through the fence and be found teed up could have resulted only from the hand of the good Lord or one of the red-sweatered caddies roaming the course."

The Pickpocket
1936 U. S. Open

In the boldest crime ever perpetrated during a major golf tournament, a sticky-fingered spectator picked the pocket of player Les Madison as he walked down the fairway!

But there's a bizarre twist. Although Madison lost an undisclosed amount of money, the real victim was actually fellow competitor Lighthouse Harry Cooper. "The gallery and [the theft] cost me the Open," declared Cooper.

Cooper was burning up the Baltusrol course in the final round of the 1936 U. S. Open. Playing at a record-setting pace, he looked like a sure winner. Even fellow competitor Johnny Bulla thought so. On the 15th hole, Bulla told Cooper, "Harry, all you've got to do to win is be standing up when you finish. You can't lose. It makes no difference what you do from here on in." But it made a big difference what a slow-moving spectator and a sneaky fingersmith did.

"The gallery started coming from all over when they heard I was winning, but there were no gallery ropes and nobody was there to handle the crowd," Cooper recalled. "People were standing in the pathway and wouldn't get out of the way on the short 16th. I said to hell with it and hit." The ball was heading straight for the pin when it struck a spectator who made a halfhearted attempt to get out of the way. The ball bounced off him into a sand trap. Instead of an easy par, Cooper had to settle for a bogey four.

Shaking off the bad break, Cooper parred the next hole. Then on the par-4 18th, he put his second shot onto the green. A par would give him a 283 and break the then U. S. Open record of 286. Cooper, whose biggest win up to then had been the 1932 Canadian Open, felt the adrenaline surge through his body. He couldn't wait to hole out. So, surrounded by spectators, he marched briskly toward the green.

Meanwhile, fellow competitor Les Madison, who also had hit his second shot onto the green, was walking with the crowd huddled around him when he felt his back pocket. "My wallet!" he shouted. "Where's my wallet?" He started to retrace his steps, thinking maybe it had fallen out, but in his heart he knew it had been swiped. He begged spectators for help in finding the pilferer, but no one had seen a thing.

Back on the green an anxious Cooper was cooling his heels. "I had to stand there for eight solid minutes before I could putt, waiting for Les," he said. "Of course, I was nervous and wanted to go. I stood there for a long while, and apparently it affected me because I three-putted from 35 feet. I wasn't mad at Les. It wasn't his fault."

Nevertheless, Cooper shot 284, a record that lasted for all of 30 minutes. While Cooper was receiving premature congratulations in the clubhouse, Tony Manero finished with a blistering 67 to snatch the victory away from him.

It was the first time in U. S. Open history when two fellow competitors felt robbed.

Ky Laffoon
Depression Era Golfer

Touring pro Ky Laffoon treated his clubs as if they were demons from Hell, punishing them for every sliced drive and torturing them for every rimmed putt.

Laffoon, a Depression-era golfer, was the first pro to average under 70 strokes in a full season on the Tour. As a tobacco-chewing, hotheaded, part-Indian nicknamed "the Chief", Ky played with fire and ice. He was prone to loud clothes and even louder invectives.

Laffoon focused most of his anger on his clubs, which he brutalized in ways more suited to the Spanish Inquisition. He drowned putters, hanged drivers, and dragged irons behind his car.

At the Jacksonville Open, for instance, Laffoon became so frustrated with his putting that, after walking off the 16th green, he began choking his putter. Then, still squeezing it at the neck of the shaft, he trod ankle-deep into a creek, shoved the club under the water, and screamed, "Drown' you poor bastard, drown!"

Whenever he played a bad round, he blamed it on his clubs for letting him down. If his disenchantment with a certain club got the best of him, he dealt it a special punishment - a ride to oblivion.

"One time Ky just putted terribly in a tournament," recalled Sam Snead. "Ol' Ky was so mad at his putter that he tied it to the back of his car and dragged it the whole way to the next tournament, four hundred miles away. When I asked him why he did it, he said that his putter deserved to be humiliated because of the way it behaved. So it bounced along there for hundreds of miles, and when we finally arrived, there was nothing left but a jagged shaft." (Before his death, Laffoon disputed the story. "It was a wedge," he said. "I was just trying to grind the edge.")

Another time, at the South Central Open in Hot Springs, Arkansas, Laffoon blew a fuse over heeling a ball with his driver. Shaking his club in a death grip, he raved, "If you can't hit the ball straight, then you should hang!" With that said, he flung the club up high into a tree, where it stuck in the fork of a branch. Once he simmered down, Ky tried to rescue the driver by throwing two more clubs up, hoping to knock it down. But they got stuck, too. Since he was playing with only seven clubs, he didn't have enough to finish the round.

Laffoon, who always played with a huge wad of tobacco stuffed in his cheek, spewed out a steady stream of juice throughout each round. The amount he spit was in direct proportion to the rise of his temper. Whenever he suffered a bad hole, he doused the bottom of the cup with a gush of tobacco juice - after first removing his ball. The player putting next would then have to reach for his ball very gingerly.

Fellow competitors stood clear of Laffoon when he began smoldering in anger, because he'd zap them with tobacco juice. Harry Cooper made the mistake of wearing an all-white outfit when he beat Laffoon in a playoff at the 1934 Western Open. By day's end, Cooper's pants were freckled with brown.

If tobacco juice wasn't pouring out of his mouth, ear-stinging foul language was during his flashes of rage. The intensity of his tirades embarrassed his wife Irene, who once threatened to leave him if he didn't curb his volatile temper. So Laffoon promised her that golf would no longer trigger a tantrum. At the next tournament, Ky seemed like a new man, totally in control, through nearly two rounds. But then his drive on the 15th hole landed in a bed of honeysuckle. After three futile swings, Laffoon let loose like a burst dam, unleashing a torrent of swear words that had spectators blushing as far away as the clubhouse. That's precisely where Irene, with her hands over her ears, was headed. Laffoon raced after her, and when he caught up with her, he said in a pleading voice, "I wasn't cussing about golf, darling. I just hate honeysuckle."

His temper caused one of the most bizarre putts in PGA history. He needed three putts from five feet to win the Cleveland Open on the last hole. But both his first and second putts lipped out of the cup. Instead of tapping in a two-incher for victory, Laffoon exploded. Not caring whether he finished first or out of the money, he slammed the putter down on the ball. Had he hit it just a small fraction of an inch to either side, he would have knocked

the ball off the course. But he hit it exactly flush on top.
The ball jumped two feet in the air - and plopped straight
in the hole.

Bobby Jones
1926 British Open

The great Bobby Jones had to pay spectator's
admission in order to play in the final round of the 1926
British Open because he forgot his contestant's badge.

It happened during a double round at the Royal
Lytham and St. Annes Golf Club, on England's west coast
north of Liverpool. After the third round in the morning,
Jones had shot 217, good for second place behind Al
Watrous, who was leading with 215. The two were then
paired for the final afternoon round.

Jones suggested that he and Watrous get away from
the clubhouse crowds during intermission and go to his
room in the nearby Majestic Hotel for a rest, a quiet lunch,
and a chance to steady their nerves. After they arrived,
the two removed their shoes and each stretched out on a
bed and tried to relax. But both were too keyed up. In
fact, they barely touched a room-service lunch of tea, toast,
and cold ham.

When they returned to the players' entrance gate to
the clubhouse, Watrous flashed his player's badge. But
Jones was stopped by the guards, who asked to see his
badge. Jones searched his pockets to no avail. Then it
dawned on him. He was so preoccupied thinking about
the final round that he had forgotten his badge, which was
back in his hotel room.

Surely someone recognized him, he said to the
clubhouse guards. After all, he was a contender in this
tournament and one of the most dominant golfers of his
era, having already been on three Walker Cup teams and
having won both the U. S. Open and the U. S. Amateur

twice. If anyone recognized Jones, he didn't admit it.

No amount of pleading from Watrous or Jones could convince the guards that Jones was a contestant. No badge, no entry; it was as simple as that. Finally, with tee off rapidly approaching, the frustrated Jones told Watrous to go on in. Knowing that he didn't have enough time to go back to the hotel and retrieve his badge, Jones figured there was only one other way to gain entrance - pay for it. So he walked over to another gate, stood in line with the spectators, and paid the common admission charge of several shillings.

Once on the course, Jones didn't need any badge to prove he was one of the world's best golfers. In the final round, he shot 74, four better than Watrous, to capture the British Open, 291 to 295.

Cyril Walker - Slowest Player in Golf
1930 Los Angeles Open

Cyril Walker was the slowest player in pro golf. He made inchworms seem like speed demons. Walker was so pokey he should have changed his name to crawler.

His maddening dillydallying drove players and tournament officials nuts. The one time he moved fast was when police hustled him off the course at the 1930 Los Angeles Open after he was disqualified for slow play.

Walker, a slight 130 pound Englishman who won the 1924 U. S. Open, played the first round at the Riviera Country Club like he always did as if he were strolling along the banks of the Avon stopping to smell the flowers. What took his competitors three hours to play took him five hours.

In the second round, his tarrying became intolerable. Before each approach shot, Walker lived up to his name by leisurely walking the hundred yards or so to the green and then sauntering back to his ball. Next, he felt the grass around the ball and picked up imaginary pebbles, leaves, and tiny pieces of cut grass. Then he took several practice swings with different clubs. Once he selected the right one, he took his stance, waggled the club at least a dozen times, and finally hit the ball.

Walker's dawdling created an enormous traffic jam for those playing behind him. The marshals tried to hurry him along, but he remained oblivious to their pleas. At the sixth hole, a tournament official warned him that if he didn't speed up, he'd be disqualified. Walker glared at the official and snarled, "You won't disqualify me. I'm Cyril Walker, a former U. S. Open champion. I've come 5,000 miles to play in your diddy-bump tournament, and I'll play as slow as I damn well please."

When he eventually arrived at the ninth hole nearly an hour later than he should have he was informed that he had been disqualified for slow play.

"The hell I am!" Walker snapped. "I came here to play, and I'm going to play!" He shoved the official aside and headed for the green to putt. The official, determined to stick to his guns, then summoned two burly policemen to escort Walker off the course. They asked him politely to leave, but the arrogant golfer just scoffed at them, believing they would never lay a hand on a former U. S. Open champion. He was wrong.

The two cops grabbed Walker by the elbows and carted him off as he kicked and screamed in protest. They dumped him at the clubhouse door and told him not to come back or he'd be swinging his clubs behind bars.

From then on most pros on the tour refused to play with Walker or behind him. So accommodating tournament officials often let him play alone with only his caddie and scorer by his side. And there was one other concession. They always sent Walker off last.

CHAPTER X

Golf Past and Present

Lest anyone think this chapter is intended to express a desire to return to the "good 'ol days", let me say as one who lived through our nation's Great Depression and World War II, that overall, America except for the marked decline in standards of moral and ethic principles in the last half century is a vastly improved nation in which to live. More than ever before, it's a great time to be alive.

As one of the twenty-four million amateur golfers in America, I'd like share with you in this portion of the book some of my observations about golf as it was played in Johnny Goodman's era compared to the game today. The observations were made over a period of time dating back to the 1932 Walker Cup Team matches and the 1934 National Amateur. The observations extend to the present and draw on my experience as a member of the gallery of all the major men's and women's golf championships, national and international, at one time or another in my life.

As a bit of an aside, as we take a look at the state of golf's progress in our modern world, we need to be reminded that what is sometimes considered progress is not really progress at all. What comes to mind is an experience I had that has no relation to golf other than that I was trying to get a catalogue number to assign to this book. The experience does make a point. An experience that was frustrating, yet humorous. Many of you, I am sure, can identify with it.

Recently, I spent 45 minutes trying to reach an "800" number. Wouldn't you know it - I got an automated system. After jumping through all the hoops (e.g., punch in your ZIP Code; punch in or say your mother's maiden name; punch in your 16-digit account number; if you know the extension number, punch that in; etc.), I got a synthesized voice saying "Your call is very important to us. Please stay on the line. Your call will be answered in the order in which it was received." I heard this message 16 times over the next 20 minutes. I finally concluded that my call was not very important, especially to them. Such systems may be cost effective to organizations but not to people calling them, who must wait an interminably long time.

If and when you ever do get a live person, you frequently find either (a) you have the wrong department and must go back to square one, or (b) the nerd on the other end knows nothing about what you want.

There was a time, not very long ago, when you could pick up a receiver and get a real live person on the other end. As you peer into the future, could this be the state of affairs?

"You have reached your doctor.
If it's your head, press 1 NOW.
If it's your stomach, press 2 NOW.
If it's your heart, press 3 NOW.
If you've died while waiting, press 4 NOW
and the morgue will be over to pick you up."

Is this progress? So, this aside, let's get back to the state of golf now and then.

On the subject of golf now and then and going back a way we should recognize at the outset that the popularity and growth of golf in the United States has been the result of many factors. Great golfing events such as a young former caddie at The Country Club winning the 1913 Open as an amateur, defeating the great British professionals Vardon and Ray played a part. The great and popular performance of the legendary Bobby Jones was also instrumental. The growth of television, the expanding economy, and a host of other factors have all contributed to the popularization of golf.

We should also not overlook the impact of the development of the automobile. The automobile has changed how the landscape is experienced as well as how towns and cities have been shaped. It was the car that helped to elevate the game from a minor pastime of thousands to a major sport that now claims millions of participants. In the past, to reach golf courses one had to travel for long periods over fairly large distances. Those same distances can now be traversed in a car in a matter of minutes. So let's not take for granted the part the automobile played in the development and popularity of golf in this country.

Even President Eisenhower served to put golf up front in the national consciousness in the 1950's. He was an avid golfer, and had a green put in the back lawn of the White House. He was a member of Augusta National, site of the Masters tournament, and often vacationed there. He even had a cottage near the 18th green.

To most present-day golfers, it is difficult to fully appreciate the way in which golf was played in the 1920's to the 1930's. To have a clear picture of any historical event, one does have to first understand the background and thinking of the time; hence, this description.

Obviously, the players then did not have the advantage of modern golf equipment. Hickory shafts were succeeded by steel in the 1930's. In the 1930's there were two other major advancements in the quality of golf equipment: the ball with a wound center and the sand wedge.

It's interesting to note that the great golfer, Bobby Jones, completed his historic grand slam in 1930 while using hickory-shafted clubs. With hickory shafts, the golfers of that era had to have exquisite timing to execute the shots they wanted. The golf courses, and especially the greens, were not as manicured to perfection as most are today. The knowledgeable agronomists and golf course maintenance equipment of today simply did not exist. I can remember being paid by the club where I caddied to help weed the golf course by hand from time to time.

The present rules of golf make putting less difficult, as well. The stymie (for match play) on the green was the rule then. This was when the golfer had to pitch over the opponent's ball on the green on occasion to get the ball in the hole. Your opponent was not required to mark his ball. This rule was abolished in 1957. Also, you couldn't repair pitch marks on the green or touch your ball to clean it.

Golfers now complain at times about spike marks. Back then, the greens were not in good enough condition to notice spike marks. Today, with beautifully conditioned fairways and greens at championship venues, the golfer seldom finds a bad lie. The first time I saw the fairways at the golf course that Jack Nicklaus designed in Murifield, Ohio, where the Ryder Cup matches were recently played, they were so perfect they literally looked like greens from a distance. Murifield is rated by the PGA tour players as the best conditioned course on their tour.

Motivation to play professional golf then was certainly not generated by any commercial aspects of the tour. For example, when Ralph Guldahl finished second to Johnny Goodman in the 1933 United States Open, he received the first prize as a professional of one thousand dollars. In 1996 Steve Jones won $425,000 for his victory at the U. S. Open. Even allowing for inflation, that's quite a change. Playing professional golf then was motivated more by hunger than anything else. On the part of the player, it took a great love for and dedication to the game of golf to play as they did. Most touring pros then had to hold down a job as a club professional, in addition to playing the tour, to make ends meet. Players then couldn't give the tour the attention they can today.

Another factor to keep in mind is that compared to today's amateur and professional golfers, golfers in Goodman's era played in very few tournaments in a year's time. In 1929, the winter tour consisted of only eight tournaments. Horton Smith, winner of the 1934 Masters, won seven of those eight tournaments. The winter weather in Nebraska is less than ideal for playing golf, even down-right hostile at times. Hence, from early fall to late spring Johnny Goodman had little opportunity to play golf.

Another interesting difference in the playing of the United States Open then, as compared to today, is that the last two rounds were played on the last day, a Saturday. This was in deference to the blue laws then, which discouraged such activities on Sundays. Playing 36 holes in one day certainly tested the endurance and skill of the golfer. The advent of television and other logistical factors has undoubtedly changed this, and from a commercial standpoint, I hardly think this will ever change. In the event of a tie in the U.S. Open then, the playoff involved 36 holes. Presently, it is 18 holes.

An interesting side light is the case of the 1931 Open where Billy Burke, the eventual winner, tied George Van Elm at the end of 72 holes. They then tied again after another 36 holes. Then they played another 36 holes. Burke won by only one stroke. This was a real marathon finish over five grueling days; a real thriller.

I will confess, though, that the competition in a United States Open today is much greater than it was in the past. The depth of skillful players on the tour presently is truly awesome; that no one can deny.

One of the major changes in golf is that in the early years of golf in America, many championship golfers came from the caddie ranks, such as Francis Ouimet, who turned the golf world on its ear when he won the National Open in 1913, beating the great English professionals, Vardon and Ray. Ouimet caddied at The Country Club in Brookline and lived across from the club on Clyde Street. He was from a family of modest means. Other greats in the game of golf where a similar story could be told, in addition to Goodman, were Sarazen, Nelson, and Hogan, to mention just a few.

Now, for the most part, because of the economic value of golf carts, caddies, except for tour caddies, are pretty much a dying breed. This is true despite the efforts of the USGA and others to encourage the use of caddies. Whether the predominance of the golf cart in golf is good or bad, I don't know. Economically, golf carts mean a great deal towards the support of many clubs. Because of this, many youngsters, especially the underprivileged, may perhaps be denied an opportunity to be introduced to golf through caddieing. As a result of this trend and other factors, there are many fewer championship golfers rising from the ranks of caddies today than there were in the past.

Generally, the crop of golf talent in America now comes mainly from our universities, not from the caddie ranks. Again, you may ask yourself if a Hogan or Nelson, who caddied together at the Glen Garden Country Club in Fort Worth, Texas, would have reached such heights in the world of golf if they hadn't had an opportunity to be exposed to the game as caddies. Obviously, young university golfers are lured by rich rewards on the professional golf tour. The few who do succeed, I think, deserve their financial rewards, for many try, but very few realize their goals.

There are not only more tour events now for the pros than in the past, but the courses are now better conditioned and more of a test of golf skills than before. In the 1930's, 40's, and 50's most of the winter tour courses were not watered and the fairways, baked hard by the sun, made for lots of roll on tee shots, which made the courses effectively shorter. The greens, too, were relatively flat without many undulations, yet the coarse long grass made putting difficult and required a putter with loft to get the ball rolling. In many cases, the teeing areas consisted of rubber mats.

As an example of low scoring in that era was the 72 hole record set by Mike Souchak who was in the upper echelon of tour pros in the Texas Open in 1955 on the Brackenridge Park Course in San Antonio, Texas. It was 6,400 yards long with a par of 71. Souchak fired a record 27 under par, a PGA record that still stands today. His scores over the four rounds were 60, 68, 64, 65, for a total of 257, in the face of cold and windy conditions. He shot a record 27 for nine holes in the first round. I'm sure you'll agree, despite the condition of the course, it was a great performance.

Then as now, the championship courses where the U. S. Open and Masters are played were real tests of every phase of golf skills. To the credit of the PGA, their major event, the PGA Championship, has recently been held at top flight championship courses, which was not the case in the past. In 1949 Sam Snead won the PGA Championship in match play at the old Hermitage Country

Club in Richmond, Virginia, of which I was a member. It is a fine old course but could not measure up to the test of golf on courses where the PGA is held in this era.

Another change from the past is the supply of really outstanding amateurs. I say this with all due respect to the fine amateurs of today. An example of this point is that at the Masters in 1996 not one amateur made the 36 hole cut, let alone came close to winning the tournament. Another change from the past is that today the fine amateurs coming out of the universities or from whatever sources are lured by the tremendous rewards of the pro tour today that simply did not exist in the past. Unless one is independently wealthy, to play lots of top level tournament golf and maintain one's amateur status today is at best difficult and perhaps impossible.

Some of the great amateurs from the 1950's, all of which I had the opportunity to watch play in the Masters, were: Frank Stranahan[1] - 1947, tied for second, only two shots back of winner Jimmy Demaret, Billy Joe Patton - 1954, finished second, one shot behind Hogan and Snead, E. Harvie Ward, Jr. - 1957, finished fourth to winner Doug Ford, Ken Venturi (then an amateur) - 1954, one shot back of winner Jack Burke, and Charlie Coe - 1961, one shot back of winner Gary Player. Coe posted the lowest score ever by an amateur in the Masters. These players had age, experience, and lots of skill.

In writing of outstanding amateur records, I would be remiss not to mention our local favorite amateur here in Richmond, Virginia, Marvin (Vinny) Giles, III. Vinny is a graduate of the University of Virginia's law school

---

[1] *A valuable bit of advice for the aspiring young golfer given by Frank Stranaham was the following: "If I had a chance to live my career in golf over, I would spend twice as much time practicing putting than I did on my long game."*

and presently heads up a company that manages professional athletes such as tour stars Tom Kite and Justin Leonard, current British Open Champion.

Vinny had an outstanding career as an amateur golfer. He won the National Amateur in 1972, and finished second four times - in 1969, 1971, 1973, and 1975. He won the British amateur in 1975 and was a Walker Cup Team member in 1973. Most recently he was Captain of the World Amateur Cup Team in 1992 and Walker Cup Team in 1993.

In his prime, Giles was one of the nation's top amateur golfers. Had he chosen to devote his full time to tournament golf, I think he had the temperament and the talent to possibly win the U. S. Open as an amateur. He thrives on competition, a characteristic of champions. He still plays outstanding golf. He recently won the Virginia State Open, beating all of the professionals with a 72 hole score of 10 under par. He finished as low amateur in the 1996 U. S. Senior Open at the Canterbury Golf Club against a strong national field. In the 1996 British Senior Open played at the Royal Portrush Golf Club in Northern Ireland, he finished in a tie for 7th place, with a 72 hole score of 2 under par, against a very strong international field of professionals and amateurs. Giles is perhaps considered to be one of the premier senior amateurs in the world today.

The likelihood of an amateur now winning a major professional event is remote. The low amateur in the 1996 U. S. Open, Randy Leen, tied for 65th place and finished 13 shots behind the winner Steve Jones.

It has been 63 years to date since Johnny Goodman won the United States Open as an amateur. In my lifetime I would like to see another amateur do it. It would be upsetting for the pros, yet good for the game.

CHAPTER XI

An Historic Match Between Golf's Finest Amateurs and Professionals

This account is based on my personal interview with
outstanding championship golfer E. Harvie Ward, Jr.,
a very healthy and active 70 year old. He teaches golf at
the famous Pine Needles Lodge and Golf Club in Southern
Pines, North Carolina. Harvie says that he really enjoys
his teaching and continued association with golf.

The idea for this historic best ball match grew out
of some conversation between a group of individuals who
were dining one evening just prior to the 1956 Crosby
Invitational at Pebble Beach in Monterey, California.
Eddie Lowery was one of the people present at this dinner
table. He was a very successful automobile dealer from
San Francisco, who was an enthusiastic supporter of
amateur golfers, especially Harvey Ward and Ken Venturi.
This is the Eddie Lowery who played a part in some of
golf's great history at the Country Club in Brookline,
Massachusetts, in 1913. He was the one who caddied for
the young American, Frances Ouimet, who made golf
history when he was a 20 year old amateur by defeating
the greatest golfers in the world to win the U. S. Open.
The group he played against included the English golfers

Vardon and Ray. Lowery is the caddie portrayed in the emblematic silhouette of Frances Ouimet and a caddie that is used by the USGA on their *Golf Journal* publication and some of the golf items marketed by them.

Another individual present at this dinner was a Mr. George Coleman, who was then president of the famous Seminole Golf Club in Palm Beach, Florida. Also present were Ben Hogan and Byron Nelson, along with two amateur stars of the day, E. Harvie Ward, Jr. and Ken Venturi.

The reason Ben Hogan was at the Crosby at all that year is rather interesting. Bing Crosby had always wanted Hogan to play in his tournament, but Ben Hogan had repeatedly declined invitations to participate. This was because Hogan simply did not care to play in pro-am tournaments. Finally, Crosby prevailed upon Ben Hogan to play that year when he agreed to be Ben's playing partner. Ordinarily, Bing didn't play in his own tournament for he preferred to be available to help make the tournament run smoothly.

To provide a little background on the amateurs, let's look at their records at that time. E. Harvie Ward, Jr. won the National Amateur in 1955 and 1956, and had won the British Amateur in 1952. He won the Canadian Amateur in 1954, finished in 4th place as an amateur in the 1957 Masters, and was a strong member of the Walker Cup Team. Ward was clearly the best amateur golfer in the United States at that time. As for Ken Venturi, he was also a strong member of the Walker Cup team with a good many tournament wins in his record. As an amateur he finished second to Jackie Burke in the 1954 Masters. Venturi subsequently turned pro and won the 1964 U. S. Open at the Congressional Country Club, overcoming physical exhaustion brought about by the extreme heat and humidity. Ken Venturi is now a top golf commentator on CBS.

So, with such records, one can appreciate why Hogan and Nelson, as great as they were, didn't take their challengers too lightly. Hogan and Nelson's records are so great they hardly need to be mentioned. Suffice it to say that they were (and still are) acknowledged to be two of the greatest golfers of all time.

During the dinner, Lowery said he would back the kids (Venturi 27 and Ward 31) to a best ball match against Hogan and Nelson. Lowery succeeded in goading the pros into a match. The pros felt they needed to put the youngsters in their place. The amateurs would be playing for bragging rights. If they won, being able to boast that they had beaten two of the best pros in the world. The amateurs had everything to gain and nothing to lose. If the pros lost, their pride would have suffered immensely.

The match was on. There was to be no money involved, with the exception of some side bets by the non-golfers. Initially, arrangements were made to play the match at Pebble Beach, but then the plan was changed and the match was held at the nearby Cypress Point Golf Club. This was done at the last minute to avoid the crowds that were planning to watch the match. The match was played on a Wednesday with a very small gallery watching. No reporters were present, for it was a spur of the moment event. Not even a score card was kept. It was a beautiful day for golf, and the amateurs were in great spirits and eager to play. Knowledgeable golfers would certainly have expected the amateurs to get a good trimming by the pros.

As the match evolved, it turned out to be a real cliff-hanger. Only on one hole did the match change from even, and that was on the par 5, 10th hole, when Hogan holed a pitch shot for an eagle three. That put the pros one up. This held all the way to the 18th hole where Venturi's excellent second shot left him with a makeable putt, which he sank for a birdie three. Hogan was the only one left with a putt for a birdie. The putt was about ten feet from the hole. At that point, Nelson remarked to Hogan: "For Lord's sake Ben, sink it." Hogan sank the putt, tying the hole. The pros won the match, one up.

The play was brilliant throughout the match. The four participants had a total of 24 birdies and an eagle between them. The foursome suffered only one bogey. Hogan shot 63, nine under par, Venturi shot 65, and Nelson and Ward had 67s. The best ball of the four was 16 under par on one of the world's most difficult golf courses.

Venturi was quoted as saying: "It was the best golf I've ever seen. That's the only team that ever beat Harvie and me. We would have challenged the world. Come to think of it, that was about what we did".

Ward made some interesting comments concerning the personalities of Nelson and Hogan. He had played with them numerous times prior to this match, and had been able to get to know them well. To him, it was always an enjoyable experience to play with Hogan[1] and Nelson.

He portrayed Nelson as talkative and outgoing, as someone and you could feel comfortable with. He was someone who would always treat you with respect. As for Hogan, on the course it was his nature to be completely focused on his game, to the extent that he blocked everything else out. He had no time for small talk. Ward also said that it was for this reason that Hogan was often misunderstood. He said Hogan actually was a very humble and private person who didn't care for publicity and adulation, yet he was a gentleman in every sense of the

[1] *Ben Hogan died at the age of 84 on July 25, 1997. Certainly one of the greatest golfers of all time.*

word. Ward said he always enjoyed playing with him because it was a real educational experience. No one should pretend that Ben Hogan was faultless. However, I'd like to comment that those who are critical of Hogan's personality and character need to be reminded of the fact that when he had his near-fatal automobile accident in 1949, in which his car was hit head on in a fog by a bus, he demonstrated his inner character. In the second before the crash he flung himself in front of his wife, Valerie, to protect her. As it turned out, that act saved both of their lives.

Further reinforcing Harvie Ward's insights about Hogan is an incident related by Gary Player. He said that, when he was a young man playing in his first U. S. Open at Southern Hills in Tulsa, Oklahoma, he was paired with Ben Hogan for the first 36 holes, a great experience for Player. He said Hogan had very little to say during the round and focused entirely on his game, but was also very polite and well-mannered and, at the close of each round, would express his appreciation of the game by thanking his fellow competitor for a good round. Later, while he was sitting in the locker room, Player felt a tap on his shoulder, looked up, and there was Hogan's face looking down at him. Hogan said, "You are going to be a great player. Do you practice much?" Player responded that he did. Hogan then said, "Well, double it" and walked away to have his lunch. Gary Player said that, hearing from a player like Hogan meant a great deal to him at that point in his career.

It's an age-old debate. Can the top-flight amateur beat a top-flight professional? The typical professional tends to have more consistency, a sharper short game, and the ability to play a greater variety of shots. He or she also tends to be tougher as a result of more tournament experience, and has the ability to play well under different course conditions. These are skills that can only come about as a result of lots of tournament playing experience. It is perhaps a given that on any one day an outstanding amateur can beat the best pro. The evidence is overwhelming that the pro who plays for his living week in and week out is going to be sharper, in the long run, than the typical amateur. Evidence of this fact is plentiful. For example, the seemingly lackluster performance of amateurs in recent U. S. Open tournaments. Despite this, however, I think this exciting match played at the Cypress Club in Monterey, California, was a fascinating event. It would have been great if it had been captured on film for all of us to see and enjoy.

Again, I can't resist repeating what has already been noted before. A truly amazing feat transpired when an amateur such as Johnny Goodman, over a period of three days, beat the best pros of that time to win the 1933 U. S. Open.

CHAPTER XII

Women in the World of Golf

When golf had its beginning in the late 19th century in the United States, men golfers were definitely not in favor of women playing their game. This was simply a case of a pure chauvinistic attitude towards women by many men who played golf, which was not unusual in the context of 19th century culture. Despite this, in 1893 a group of determined ladies in New Jersey organized a course "for women only" in Morris County, New Jersey. In 1895, with the support of the newly formed United States Golf Association, they held their first National Amateur Championship at Meadow Brook, Long Island, New York. Mrs. C. S. Brown won. By the turn of the century, women had won their fight to establish golf as their game too.

Until 1945 women's golf languished, and women found it difficult to play in a game very much dominated by men. In 1946 the great woman golfer Patty Berg was the prime mover in establishing the Ladies Professional Golf Association (LPGA). Patty was the inspirational leader and the first president. She, along with the help of many others, had the energy to get women's professional golf off the ground. She had won the women's National Amateur in 1938 and the first Women's National Open in 1946, as well as many other tournaments too numerous to mention. She had the credentials, the vision, and energy to provide the leadership in women's professional golf.

In 1951 Patty Berg and Babe Dickinson Zaharias, a great golfer in her own right, played in a unique tournament called the Weathervane. They played head to head in 36 hole events throughout the country and drew tremendous galleries. This tournament played a tremendous part in popularizing golf throughout the nation. The final outcome after 180 holes was that Patty Berg won on the last hole by one stroke.

Patty Berg has put on thousands of exhibitions over the years and was, and still is, a timeless good will ambassador for women's golf. She continues to this day, having had a clinic and exhibit at the recent Women's Open Championship at Pine Needles, in Southern Pines, North Carolina. Patty Berg is undoubtably a living legend and hero of women's golf.

During its early years in the 1940's and 50's, the women's tour did not become really popular, despite the many outstanding players in its ranks. In 1940 when Patty Berg turned pro, there were only three professional events that year. It wasn't until the seventies that large companies realized that women's golf was such a potentially huge market for their products.

The LPGA now is a multimillion dollar tour with 310 professionals playing. There is a total of 20 million dollars in prize money awarded in 30 tournament events each year. The players on the LPGA are the cream of the crop of global women's golf talent.

LPGA commissioner Jim Ritts recently said that the 1997 women's tour will play 42 tournaments for 29 million dollars, quite a bit more than the 1996 schedule. The women's share of the professional spotlight is indeed growing.

Presently, there are five million women golfers in the United States - one out of every five golfers is a woman. At golf clubs and municipal courses throughout the nation women are increasingly becoming active golfers, and there are now several monthly periodicals devoted exclusively to women's golf. Accompanying this increase in popularity of golf among women is a boom in sales of women's golf equipment.

The growth of women's golf is certainly not solely a result of the growth of women's professional golf. The USGA has played in the past and continues to play a lion's share role in the popularizing of women's golf. Their development of the U. S. Women's Open, U. S. Girl's Junior, U. S. Public Links, U. S. Women's Amateur, U. S. Women's Mid-Amateur, and the USGA Senior Women's Amateur have played a tremendous role in the development of women's golf. The USGA's overall goal is to preserve the integrity and values of the game, which they have done well. Additionally, there is no doubt in my mind that excellent television coverage has been the single most important factor in the popularization of golf. Golf's popularity among women has grown tremendously on an international scale as well. Women pros are now playing tournaments in Japan, Mexico, England, Australia, and Canada.

An interesting bit of history in women's golf that has something to say for youth was when in 1971 Laura Baugh, at the age of 16, became the youngest winner of the Women's National Amateur Championship. She turned professional two years later.

At this point I'd like to give you a picture of Women's championship golf as played in the U. S. Women's Open Championship at Pine Needles Lodge and Country Club in Southern Pines, North Carolina, in 1996. This is the home course of noted professional Peggy Kirk Bell who was made honorary Chair of the tournament. One must bear in mind that championship golf and golf generally are two entirely different games. One I watch, the other I try to play.

First, here is a little background and history on the Women's Open. The first Open was played in 1946. Conducted as match play, the event was won by Patty Berg. The following year its format was changed to 72 hole stroke play, as it is played now. In contrast, the women's regular tour events are played in three rounds. All players go off the first tee at the Open, whereas in their regular tour half of the field begins play on the 1st tee and the other half on the 10th. This makes for faster play.

The format of the Women's Open is similar to the Men's Open in that the tournament is truly open to all golfers. There were a record 876 applicants to enter the U. S. Women's Open in 1996. Amateurs can attempt to qualify sectionally, provided they have a handicap of 4.4 or less. Winners of the last two National Amateurs are exempt from qualifying. The pros qualify sectionally pretty much the same way the men qualify for their Open. The last year's winner of the Ladies British Open and the two leaders of the Japanese and European tours are also invited and are exempt from qualifying; this gives the tournament an international flavor. After qualifying, the final field consisted of 135 pros and 15 amateurs.

As you can imagine, Open courses are generally greater tests of golf skills than the regular LPGA Tour courses. U. S. Open courses are set up by the USGA to have fairways only 30 yards wide and narrower on short holes; Pine Needles was no exception. The rough is usually deep, and a real penalty for those whose shots stray into it. How well the ball lies in the rough determines how well the shot can be hit. The holes are cut in the greens at least five paces from the edge of the green. Contrary to popular belief, the USGA chooses an area on the greens for the hole that is near level as possible.

Depending on the weather, the greens can be hard as marble and lightening fast. At Pine Needles the green speeds were measured as 11 on the Stempmeter - that's real fast and equal to the speed of the greens at the men's Open. The fairways are cut closely so that the players can spin the second shots to better hold the greens.

It goes without saying that effective course management always plays a major role in scoring at the Open. The fact that those players with 8 over par for the first two rounds made the 36 hole cut attests to the difficulty of Pine Needles.

Pine Needles was designed by the famous golf course architect Donald Ross. It was built in 1927 and is an outstanding test of golf. The course is 6207 yards long with a par of 70, and includes some tough par 4's. Many of the green surfaces are designed in a dome shape to facilitate drainage, but at the same time, this makes putting on the greens all the more difficult. Many of the greens looked like a coffee cup turned upside down. In many cases, if your approach shot to the green goes too far to the left or right of the flagstick your ball will roll off the green and go down a slope. If it goes beyond the flagstick, it will roll off the back edge down a slope. In any event leaving the player with an extremely difficult shot to the flagstick to make par. Many of the players in this Open carried 6, 7, and 9 woods to hit their second shots to the green; this way they could hit the ball higher and better hold the green than if they used long irons. In many cases, to be in a position to putt, it was imperative to keep the ball below the flagstick on the approach shot into the green.

Drives at this Open course had to be hit to the part of the fairway that put them in a good position for second shots. Again, calling for real accuracy.

My overall experience of watching the tournament was very pleasant. The players were generally very friendly and approachable, which can't always be said of the men pros. Pine Needles was in superb condition with lush fairways, lots of tall pines to avoid, and perfectly conditioned greens. The weather throughout the tournament made for pleasant watching, although I'm sure the players would have liked a little rain to help soften the greens.

Women want to win the Open more than any other tournament, and this sentiment was reflected in their serious demeanor. The galleries were big, excited, and enthusiastic. It is interesting that there were lots of men in the gallery. I expect they can learn more from the women than they can from the men pros. By this I mean that, since the men pros play such a long game, it is difficult for the average golfer, man or woman, to translate that into what they experience in their game. In my opinion the women are just as accurate as the men and play a short game every bit equal to that of the men pros.

As usual, some comments from the gallery were quite humorous. Two I think are worth repeating. While watching the pros trying to decide which club to use on a par three, someone in the gallery remarked, "I don't have that problem. Regardless of the length of the hole, I always use a driver." Another said, "After seeing them play, I've decided to give up the game."

For the most part, the players' swings were beautifully fluid and orthodox. They depend on rhythm and tempo to generate power. The only difference I see between the men and women pros is that the men are simply stronger and consequently can hit the ball farther.

However, the length these women achieve off the tee is very impressive. The long hitters like Laura Davis and Michelle McGann hit it about 260 yards off the tee, and most average 230 to 240 yards. Except for the long par 5's and 4's, distance was not a big factor in this Open. Pine Needles, the pros agree, is not a course you can play aggressively - keeping the ball in play, accuracy, a razor sharp short game, with superior putting ability, is the name of the game as it often is in championship golf.

Unfortunately, the tournament was plagued with slow play. Five and one half hour rounds were common. On the second day, one group took 63 minutes to play the first three holes. Needless to say, this played on the nerves of the players.

It was an exciting Open, especially since the winner, Annika Sorenstam played superb golf throughout. Her background prior to winning the 1996 Open was remarkable. Prior to winning the 1995 Women's Open she won six times on four continents and became the first woman to lead both the American and European tours in earnings in the same year. She won the World Championship of Women's Golf and won an LPGA tournament in St. Louis by 10 strokes. She won the Vare Trophy for lowest scoring average and Player of the year in 1995. In her native Sweden she received their prestigious sports award, Athlete of the Year.

Her final round 66 for a total of 272 was six strokes ahead of her closest pursuer. This was a record for the oldest tournament in women's professional golf. She missed only five fairways off the tee in 72 holes - her accuracy was simply brilliant.

This was the second consecutive year this 25 year old from Sweden has won the U. S. Women's Open, and she has been on the tour only three years. Annika was not one of the big hitters off the tee in the Open. She hit it about 240 yards, but her deadly accuracy paid off. It was interesting to note that she carried five woods in her bag.

She made an eagle in the last round on the par 5 10th hole by hitting a 210 yard three wood to the green and holing a 20 foot putt. She normally displayed all of the emotions of an iceberg, but with this, she flashed a smile and thrust both arms in the air. She had a double bogie on the back side of the final round, but refused to falter. She proceeded to birdie the 15th and 16th holes. She finished and won the first prize of $212,500.

She said at the close "Whatever I did, I seemed to do right. My shots were straight, my putts went in. It was as if nothing was in the way. I guess it was just my day. I almost felt like I could close my eyes and hit it. It wasn't going to matter." What did matter was that she won with a day-long display of poise and skill.

In closing this chapter, I think we can safely say that today, women's feet are firmly planted in the world of golf.

CHAPTER XIII

More Golf History and Observations on Golf and Golf Tournaments Today

International Golf

Without a doubt, golf is now becoming a worldwide competitive sport. There is now even a golf course in Russia, and in China the first golf tournament has recently been played. It is a fact that in recent years European golfers have dominated many of our major championships and are now giving our Ryder Cup Team stiff competition, with the Europeans winning the cup in 1995 (However, the European Ryder Cup Team used to only include players from Great Britain). Further evidence of this is that the United States players have won the Masters only twice out of the last nine years. There is one school of thought that says this is so perhaps because their golfers are a tougher breed, having to struggle more to arrive where they are. This, of course, is a debatable subject, but I don't think one can deny that our leading professionals are somewhat spoiled by all the special attention that's given to them. But at the same time I think it's very encouraging that more and more of our players are playing in the British Open and that the American, John Daly, won the championship in 1995.

My observation as an amateur golfer watching the British Open being played at the Royal Lytham and St. Annes in England in July, 1979, the year Ballesteros won, was that the game played in Britain is entirely different from the game in this country. The primary factors in this difference are the weather and the design of the golf courses. I had to wear a borrowed overcoat to watch in the wind and cold and be reasonably comfortable. Remember that the British Open is played in July. What struck me, too, as being markedly different in the golf there was the more natural appearance of the course. A greater challenge from the wind and cold was present, and surely their bunkers were so much more severe and penalizing. In some cases, it looked like you had to go down on a ladder to get to your shot. Obviously, too, the player has to call on his imagination more in the execution of his shots - lots of bump and run shots are called for.

How golfers in the British Open that year played so well under the conditions of the course and the wind and cold is more than I can understand. The tournament had set up bars in tents throughout the course, and I might say, they were getting lots of attention, considering the wind and cold. Another difference from America was the legal betting on the tournament. The bookies had the odds down pretty well - better, I think, than the sports writers.

In Britain the British Open is referred to simply as the Open, since it is the original Open golf tournament. In 1996 the 125th Open was held. I might say that the galleries in Britain are especially knowledgeable of golf and are very appreciative of the caliber of play they witness at the Open.

I thought it was interesting that in the evening, when I went to dinner in the lovely little village of St. Annes, the restaurant where I dined seated one at a big round table with others. There I met and chatted with ardent and knowledgeable golfers from throughout the world - a great custom and wonderful experience.

It is interesting to note that in 1996 the British Open was again held at the Royal Lytham and St. Annes course. The weather conditions for this Open were entirely different from those of the 1979 British Open: sunny with temperatures in the 80's. The greens were slower and holding reasonably well, and there was very little wind. Shots were into hard fairways making for lots of roll when the ball landed. This made for a short course, but called for great accuracy to avoid the penalizing pot bunkers.

The World Amateur Cup played with competition between teams representing countries throughout the world definitely promotes the game for amateurs on an international scale.

Another ongoing development for international golf is the World Cup of Golf for professionals. In 1996 this event was held at Somerset West in South Africa. There were 32 nations represented, including such countries as Venezuela and China. The United States team came into the 1996 matches with four consecutive wins. In 1996 the South African team of Ernie Els (1994 U. S. Open winner) and Wayne Westner swamped the field by 18 shots during four days of wind, rain, sun, and overcast. Els was 16 under par for the four days and Westner was 13 under. Tom Lehman and Steve Jones of the United States finished second. It was the largest margin of victory since Ben Hogan and Sam Snead lead the U. S. team to victory in this event. A gallery of over 8000 attended in 1996, the largest ever for this event. This is yet another example of the growing popularity of golf throughout the world, as well as the fact that the United States no longer dominates the field.

The President's Cup Tournament

The President's Cup was inaugurated in 1994 by the Professional Golfer's Association Tour to capitalize on the popularity of the established Ryder Cup. It's a three day competition patterned after the Ryder Cup format. It matches a 12 member team from the United States against a 12 member International team that excludes the European Ryder Cup team members. In the inaugural event the United States routed the International team by a wide margin. In 1996, the competition for the United States was much stiffer in that the International team was strengthened by such players as Greg Norman, Ernie Els, and Steve Elkington. Arnold Palmer captained the United States team and Peter Thompson, five time British Open Champion, captained the International team.

The teams play four ball matches (the best ball of each team prevails), foursome matches (the best ball of each team playing alternate shots), and single matches (one player playing against another). All matches are played as match play. Each match is worth a point. A total of 32 points are at stake, $16^{1}/_{2}$ points are required for victory.

In Ryder Cup play, in the event of a tie, the defending champions keep the Cup. If there is a tie in the President's Cup matches, each team captain selects one player, and these two play a head to head match to determine the winning team. This did not happen in 1996, but one can imagine that such a match would be quite dramatic, to say the least.

The match play format makes for exciting golf - especially in the foursome matches (alternate shot) where there is a lot of consultation between players. In the foursome matches as well as the four ball matches, there is enormous pressure on the players in that they are trying to satisfy their partners. In the single matches the type of psychological pressure and playing strategy are different than in the usual medal play format. For the gallery, all of the matches are fascinating to watch. Overall, this format of play is a refreshing change from watching the typical medal play format of the regular tour.

In 1996 there were so many thrilling matches that it's difficult to single one out. Yet one match that was especially sensational was between the power hitter Greg Norman and the bull dog competitor Corey Pavin. Norman, the former British Open Champion and Pavin, the former U. S. Open Champion, were both at the top of their games.

On the last day, on the par 5, 12th hole, Norman outdistanced Pavin by 60 yards off the tee. Pavin was in a bunker 50 yards from the green in two. Norman was on in two, putting for an eagle. Pavin knocked his third shot within a few feet of the hole. Norman had a putt of about 60 feet. He hit his putt about 7 feet past the hole, missed that putt, and took a par 5 for the hole. Pavin sank his putt for a birdie and a win. As is often said, when Pavin is within 100 yards of the hole you're going to have your hands full playing against him. Norman finally won the match 3 and 1, but he sure had his hands full. I would say that it was the most breathtaking golf I've ever had the opportunity to watch. Never have I seen so many great golf shots - it was pure golf, that's for sure.

The 1996 matches were played at the par 72, 7289 yard Robert Trent Jones Golf Club in northern Virginia, not far from Washington, D. C.. The gallery included former President Bush, Co-Chairman of the event, as well as President Clinton, an avid golf fan. It is an unusual course setting in that it is not surrounded by housing developments. The course, in superb condition, is on Lake Manassas, and is in a superbly beautiful setting. The course, designed by Jones, is a test of championship golf, and demands the use of every club in the bag. The greens have lots of contour and a fast pace - difficult to putt. To stray from the fairway meant being in deep rough.

On the last day of the tournament, the last match of the day, Fred Couples and Vijay Singh were on the 16th tee and everyone else had finished. The teams were tied at $15^{1}/_{2}$ points each. Couples was 2 up. Singh promptly birdied the par 3, 16th by hitting a beautiful 8 iron to within a foot of the hole, and won the hole to pull within one down with two holes to go. Both golfers hit the fairway with their drives on the par 4 17th hole and the green with their secondshots. Couples was about 25 feet from the hole and Singh about 10 feet closer. Afterwards Couples said "When I got there, the putt really wasn't that hard from the standpoint of rolling up there and trying to two-putt". Couples judged the speed perfectly and the ball went into the center of the cup. He leapt into the air with excitement. After things settled down Singh putted. With such pressure I'm sure that to him the hole must have looked about the size of a shirt button. His ball hit a spike mark about five feet from the hole and missed. The United States won by one point. Couples was the hero of the day. The gallery went wild.

Peter Thompson, the International Team Captain said at the close, "I'm emotionally drained after such a day as today. The last hour has been almost heart-stopping for us. What a contest. I can't remember in my lifetime anything as exciting and emotional as this. It was our deep wish that we could make such a contest of it, that it would insure the perpetuation and growth of the event; and I think we must have done that surely".

This year's tournament was exhilarating to watch with a breathtakingly close finish. My prediction is that this new tournament on the golfing scene will become one of the premier golfing events in the world.

Scores Now and Then

A s you perhaps know, the Vardon Trophy is awarded each year to the professional golfer who has the lowest round average. Actual scores and rounds recorded started in 1947. That first year, almost 50 years ago, the trophy went to Jimmy Demaret, three-time winner of the Masters, with 92 rounds played at an average score for 18 holes of 69.90. The Vardon Trophy Award went to Steve Elkington in 1995, with 72 rounds played and an average score of 69.59, hardly a big difference. Unquestionably, to compare actual scores even on the same golf course is difficult, for weather, condition of the course, how it is set up for play, such as speed of greens, and on and on, make direct comparisons of scores across the years difficult. Yet, I think this Vardon Trophy record, with less than one-half a stroke difference almost 50 years apart, is telling.

Another interesting observation is that in the 1933 U.S. Open, Johnny Goodman won with a one under par on a tough championship course of 6,927 yards. Compare that score to Corey Pavin's. In 1995 when he won the U.S. Open on the 100th Anniversary of the USGA on one of the finest courses in America, Schinnecock; Pavin's score was even par.

Great Golf Courses

T he great East Course of the Merion Golf Club in Ardmore, Pennsylvania, has been the venue for many national championships. Jack Nicklaus described it this way: "Acre for acre, it may be the best test of golf in the world." It isn't brutally long at 6,544 yards, but has strategic variation in hole lengths - from 129 yards to 600 yards. Despite its lack of length, it requires play with lots of finesse, as all championship courses do. It has small greens and strategically placed hazards; it is a shot-makers challenge. The greens are undulating for the most part, making for a premium on putting. The pins don't have flags, but wicker baskets on the top, used in days past for golf maintenance personnel to keep their lunches. With no flags, you can't tell which way the wind is blowing. Merion is renowned for its 16th, 17th, and 18th holes, each of which crosses an old quarry. The blind tee shot on the 18th, which Hogan mastered with two identical shots in two days during his Open victory there in 1950, is a very challenging shot.

Merion is old and was a challenge to golfers of yesteryear, yet remains a great challenge for the modern champion today. It's an example of the kind of place where golf was intended to be played. Perhaps there need to be more championship courses like it. Obviously, there are many others of equal caliber. This is just to illustrate one.

I had the pleasure of playing the great Dornoch course in northern Scotland, which is another example of an old but great test of golf. The Royal Dornoch Golf Club, founded in 1855, is considered one of the greatest links on Earth. Links is a form of golf course in Scotland laid out upon windswept land by the sea, with many natural hazards. Links golf was the original form of the game. The weather in Scotland can be very capricious with rain squalls and wind coming up very suddenly. Scots often say that if you don't like the weather just wait a little while.

Dornoch is a classic, completely natural course whose character changes with the wind. Set on the edge of Embo Bay, on public land, the course is a municipal meeting place, where golfers mingle with residents walking their dogs and children riding bikes through fairways. My play there made it clear to me that golf in Scotland as compared to golf in America can be two different games. On some of the holes, I was playing with a 30 mile an hour wind directly in my face. You had to lean forward at times to stand up. No one had to explain to me why they were using a smaller size ball at the time. Needless to say, I enjoyed the round even though I spent a lot of time in the heather and the pot bunkers. An interesting sidelight is that Donald Ross, the eminent golf course architect who emigrated from Dornoch, Scotland, around the turn of the century, designed some 600 courses in the United States, including the famous Pinehurst No. 2 in Pinehurst, North Carolina, where he ultimately lived.

Back in 1974 when I was able to play many of the courses in Scotland, it's interesting to note that the fee for many was less than a dollar for a day's play. For the most part, their courses are simply for golf - no tennis courts, swimming pools, or elaborate club houses.

Shot-Making Today and Yesterday

An often overlooked characteristic of a fine championship golfer is his ability to judge distances accurately and to translate that into club selection, thereby getting the ball close enough to the flagstick to make the birdie putts necessary for low scores.

The modern pro's ability, depending on the lie, to maneuver the ball - fades, draws, high or low - is very impressive. Most of the pros hit their drives with a high fade. The object is to have the ball land softly, making it less likely to roll into trouble as compared to a draw which tends to roll more after landing. Fading the ball also makes a lot of sense for another reason. If you aim down the center of a fairway 50 yards wide you only allow yourself 25 yards on either side before you find yourself in difficulty. Yet, if you can hit to the left side of the fairway and fade the ball you have 40 yards to work with. As good as the pros are, even they can't always do this. Despite the advantages of fading the ball, there are pros who regularly hit the ball with a right to left trajectory and are quite successful with that type of shot.

At the major tournaments the courses call for position golf off the tee and for second shots to the greens. This is to put the player in the best position to two putt or one putt on lightning fast greens. Accuracy is the name of the game, especially when hitting approach shots to championship greens at major events. Three putting, for example, at the Masters, is not at all unusual for even the best professionals. On downhill putts, barely breathing on the ball can put it in motion. Also, the ability to read all types of greens, Bermuda, bent grass, etc., on a different course every week is all important to the success of the professional golfer. Most of us playing the same course every week don't even begin to encounter such problems.

Even for the pros, despite good mechanics and ability to read greens for line and speed, putting is an especially elusive part of the game. Success at putting can suddenly disappear, for no apparent mechanical reason, and this can eat away at a player's confidence level. This can even happen to the best players. Then it will all come back and they're off and running again. Putting skills can be elusive and, in fact, putting is almost like another game altogether. Many a major championship has been lost when a contender's putting ability has left them on the last few holes.

Weather conditions obviously have a great bearing

on scores as well. Wind can be unpredictable and affect shots in unpredictable ways. The average golfer often overlooks that the tour pro has to play in the face of adverse weather conditions such as high winds, cold, and rain, while the average amateur at such times remains in the club house playing gin rummy. This is so apparent on the short par three 12th at Augusta National - Amen Corner. This hole has proven to be Waterloo for many a player, with its small narrow green that becomes nearly impossible to hit with any wind blowing. Wind obviously not only makes it difficult to control the ball, it also creates a problem for the player in maintaining rhythm and balance. In the wind the championship player has to have the ability to hit knock down shots in order to counteract the wind's effect. The wind can even affect putting. In general, however, outstanding players have the ability to shape their shot regardless of conditions.

There is a great debate as to whether or not the top players of today are better shot-makers than those of the past. Personally, I think that it's impossible to fairly compare players from the two different eras. You have to take into account a myriad of factors - prize money, equipment, conditions of the golf course, and on and on.

I think an interesting set of statistics gathered by a noted sports writer addresses the argument concerning whether or not today's golf stars are better golfers than those from the past. The achievements of great golfers during two ten year periods, 1941-1950 and 1986-1995 were compared. From 1941 to 1950, Ben Hogan won 51 tournaments on the PGA Tour, Sam Snead won 39 tournaments, and Byron Nelson won 38. Now for the comparison with the big winners on the PGA Tour over the last ten years. Greg Norman and Nick Price each have 13 wins. Corey Pavin, Tom Kite, and Paul Azinger have

11 wins each. Finally, Fred Couples, Ben Crenshaw, Curtis Strange, Davis Love, III have nine wins apiece.

This writer went on to respond to the statement that competition is tougher now than in the past by stating the fact that normally only 30 players can win a golf tournament in any era. The other players in the field realize they have little chance of winning.

What I do think is true is that the very top players of yesteryear compare favorably with the present day top players, whether it's Ouimet, Jones, Hogan, or Nicklaus. I think the reason for this is that, at the very top level of golf, at a caliber of golf that sets the few apart from the rest, golf primarily becomes a mind game. Dedication, ability to concentrate and execute under pressure, and golf course management, these are what has separated the greats from the field in the past and does so in the present as well. Ben Hogan said that championship golf is 20% ability and 80% golf course management. An example of Ben Hogan's ability to concentrate comes from a round at the Masters. Hogan, paired with Byron Nelson, was playing the par three 12th at Augusta National. Nelson, with a brilliant iron, had a hole in one. When recording Byron Nelson's score after play on the hole was finished, Hogan asked, "What did you have there?" Nelson, surprised, said, "I had a hole in one!"

Johnny Goodman's view was that "You have to take one shot at a time and have great patience in order to perform well." This advice certainly applies for all time. Also, there is the need to hit a variety of shots - fades, drives, and shots with various types of trajectory. When the best golfers have played a poor shot or hole, they can control their emotions and faculties. As the pressure mounts the champion is able to keep his swing and game together and is able control his thoughts and emotions.

They have an inner belief that they can win against anyone.

A good example of this is observed at the practice tee at a major tournament - all the players look alike performance-wise. Yet, when they are out on the course and faced with a down-hill, side-hill, lightening fast, four-foot putt or some other difficult shot, do they pull it off or not? Some can and some can't. Again, it's a mind game at that level of golf, especially in the area of putting.

Hard Work, Toughness, and Luck

There is no question in my mind that some element of luck can enter into the winning of a championship. Winning or not winning can sometimes amount to only a razor's edge difference, like a ball that kicks left onto the green from the bank of a water hazard, when if it had kicked right, would have been in the water. There are times when a winner who overcomes bad breaks on the way almost seems like he or she was destined to win.

One example of the dedication and the ability to work harder than the next guy is an experience I'll never forget. While attending the Masters in Augusta during a very cold spring day a good while ago, I went out to the practice tee on a chilly, rainy afternoon and found only one golfer out there working on his game. That was Ben Hogan. In my opinion, Hogan had the will to do what the other guy wouldn't.

To think that by just spending a lot of time on the practice range and working hard that anyone can become a great golfer is ludicrous. In my opinion a golfer, like any other athlete, has a certain amount of innate ability. When they reach the full level of that ability, no amount of work will cause them to exceed that ability level. I think that truly great golfers have the capacity for greatness. For the most part, championship golfers achieve pretty close to what their ability has allowed them to achieve.

The really great championship players of the past did whatever it took to win - they had the ability to rise to the occasion regardless of the circumstances. There are many, many examples of this. One that comes to mind was that of Ben Hogan's meeting the challenge of winning the British Open in 1953 at Carnoustie in Scotland. This was the year he won the U. S. Open and the Masters.

On the persuasion of his friends that he needed to complete his career by playing in the British Open, he made a trip to Great Britain for the first time. He went over well before the time of the tournament and meticulously studied the course and adapted his swing to the hard turf. In the evenings he walked the holes backwards until he memorized the natural features and planned his strategy. He won the tournament with rounds of 73-71-70-68, for a 72-hole total of 282.

To quote the great English golf writer, Bernard Darwin, "Hogan gave you the impression that he was capable of getting whatever score was needed to win." The way in which Hogan won this tournament is one of the most amazing feats in the history of golf. Hogan never returned to the British Open. I think his winning the British Open is a clear example of a champion's ability to do whatever is necessary to win. This same ability is characteristic of today's great champions as well.

It needs to be said though, that a human being, regardless of his abilities or desires, cannot sustain a winning performance time after time. There have to be down periods such as when the great Bobby Jones was defeated in 1929 at Pebble Beach, California, in the first round of the National Amateur by unknown Johnny Goodman, the 20 year old amateur.

Modern Technology Meets Golf

A negative of modern golf that takes away from the original challenge is the distance the modern ball travels. This is an age old discussion in golf. First a few facts on this subject. In 1976 the USGA adopted an Overall Distance Standard Test which allows for balls to travel 296.8 yards when hit by Iron Byron on the USGA driving range. In 1995 there were more than 200 balls tested and approved that were within five yards of that standard. The PGA Tour recently started measuring the length of drives on two holes of tour events. The average drive of the pros was 260 yards and since then the average has remained almost the same. The median driving distance on the Senior PGA tour in 1995 was 253 yards, almost 10 yards less than the average driving distance on the regular PGA tour. Despite all of these facts and figures, the discussion continues - should there be a reduction in the distance the ball travels?

The USGA maintains a current list of approved golf balls and only those on the list can be played in USGA tournament events. An interesting note related to approved golf balls occurred in the 1996 Hartford Open. Greg Norman, to his credit, disqualified himself after two rounds when he was very much in contention after discovering that the ball he had played, which in fact conformed to USGA rules, was labeled incorrectly and thus was not on the USGA list.

Top pros now generate tremendous club head speed at impact, and some can hit the ball over 280 yards. At the Masters in 1996, one pro on the 15th hole, without wind, hit a drive of 360 yards. This has made many holes, particularly par 5's, obsolete on some courses unless they have room to expand. With all due respect to the USGA

with their control over design of equipment and balls, I
do wonder if perhaps there needs to be some solution to
the problems all of this increased distance has created.
To watch a pro play on television at regular tour events on
a long par five with a driver and a 200 yard six iron and
reach the green in two leaves me puzzled. Another
example of this was when, in the 1996 Masters, some of
the golfers on the par five 15th hole, 500 yards, reached
the green with a drive and a seven iron with no wind behind
them. You have to wonder if this hole is really a par five.
There's no question the modern pro's strength and
beautifully timed and orthodox swing with improved
equipment play a big part in all of this extra distance, but
when a touring pro of some 20 years past claims he's
hitting the ball further today even though he's much older,
I feel that some more serious attention needs to be paid to
this issue. I understand the courses are not as easy as
these players make them look, but at times, they do make
playing golf on them seem as easy as shelling peas.

On the other side of the argument for reducing the
distance the ball is traveling is the fact that in the last 40
years average distance has increased only ten yards. Some
of this added distance could be the result of better
equipment, the changes in the length and loft of clubs,
improved maintenance of the firmer fairways, not to
mention bigger and stronger golfers. Most of the pros
swing a club so smoothly that the club looks as though
it's a part of their body. There is no question that the
improvement in scores has come to a great extent as a
result of the tremendous improvement in the pro's ability
to score around and on the greens and not the distance
they hit the ball.

The two piece golf ball for the most part has been
marketed for the average amateur golfer. Some companies

have recently developed a two piece ball for the professional. Some pros claim these balls retain the same feel and consistency of a regular ball, but roll better on the greens. This is yet another example of how technology has affected the caliber of play in modern golf.

With all the complications involved, I doubt that the USGA, the Royal & Ancient, the PGA, and the LPGA can do any more than they are doing to restrict the distance the ball travels. I will say, as a poor amateur, as I grow older my drives are getting shorter, so certainly this whole subject is not one of my problems. In fact, I'm looking for ways to make the game easier, not more difficult.

The use of the golf glove is a fairly new development. Even players in later years such as Ben Hogan never used a glove for their left hands. Now those players using gloves far outnumber those who don't. It unquestionably helps the player to better control the club. It's interesting that golfers remove their glove to give them better feel while they are putting.

Another change today is the development of the extra length putter used on the senior tour as well as by some on the regular tour. Transporting the extra long putter, as you could well imagine, might be problematic. In view of this, the USGA has allowed the putter to be made in two pieces that can be reassembled before play, much like a pool cue, so that it can be more easily transported. There has been some speculation that it may, in the future, be ruled out for use by the USGA, because many players anchor the butt of the putter to their chest in order to swing the putter like a pendulum.

A great positive change in golf from the years past is the tremendous improvement in golf instruction methods. The video camera has been particularly effective. The result of this improvement is reflected in the fact that top amateurs and pros, with very few exceptions, have beautiful orthodox swings. Today, the techniques of golf and the golf swing are approached by the professional as a science. Walter Hagen, and others from the past, with the unorthodox swings they had, would surely be oddities on the PGA Tour today. Most pros, though, would have liked to have had Hagen's temperament.

Another plus for the touring pros that wasn't present in the past is the availability of the physical fitness center that travels with them. I've had a chance to inspect one, and they are marvelous. There is no doubt that the modern touring pro, overall, is more conscious of his physical fitness and strength, and it shows very clearly in how far they hit the ball. As an aside, I'd like to say that it's possible for a 40 year old pro to condition himself to attain the physical capabilities of a 20 year old. However, a 20 year old could never attain the experience-filled mind of a 40 year old. So much said for the value of experience.

Overall, I think the USGA does a great job at the difficult task of making sure that technology doesn't replace skill in the game, thus preserving the integrity of golf.

The Explosion of Golf Instruction

Compared to the past, the availability and mass-marketing of golf instruction during the past decade is tremendous. Instructional videos and books from the top tournament players proliferate today. Now there is even a cable television network devoted exclusively to golf. Computer users can even obtain golf instruction on the Internet. These fairly recent developments are bound to have a positive effect on the popularity of golf. All of this instructional information helps the average golfer to play better and enjoy golf more.

For the young avid golfer it means developing a more orthodox swing and a better overall game. Tiger Woods has had access to excellent instruction from the very beginning. As golf great and television commentator Johnny Miller recently commented, "Tiger Woods has the most technically perfect golf swing I've ever seen. Tiger's swing is a computer model for precision and conformity." In the future, I think more than ever most of the top players will all have look-alike orthodox swings. The unorthodox swings exemplified by Walter Hagen and Lee Trevino will, for the most part, be things of the past.

Getting Around the Course

Another negative is that golf has turned into a riding game instead of a walking game. The economic value of the golf cart has made it that way, and I don't think it will change. I'm glad to see, though, that the USGA doesn't permit the use of carts in their championship, and I hope this rule prevails. The only exception made by the USGA to this was that, since 1969, carts are allowed in the National Senior Amateur Tournament. Carts are allowed largely because caddies are difficult to obtain in the autumn when school has resumed. In the past, they played the final 36 holes on the last day of the U.S. Open. Surely a player on that level should be able to get around 18 holes on the last day walking.

Slow play today is a real problem, whether it's in a tournament or a friendly weekend round. Slow play is really tough on the tour player whose temperament leads him to play faster. I know in championship golf, especially, it's not unusual for players to take five or six hours to complete a round. This seems like an inordinately long time to complete 18 holes of golf. Exposure on television, as wonderful as it is, has spilled over to the average golfer in that he tends to emulate the pros in the time they take to play. In 1987, according to the National Golf Foundation, an average player on an average public course took three hours 50 minutes to play 18 holes. In 1992 a round took over four hours. Before golf carts and housing developments surrounding golf courses there was little distance between greens and the next tee. However, this distance has become increasingly greater on modern golf courses, and it takes quite a long time on some of these layouts to walk from green to tee. This phenomenon has further necessitated the use of golf carts.

I've watched Gene Sarazen play at the Masters in Augusta, Georgia, and his speed of play was remarkable. Someone reported that in 1972 at Marco Island, Florida, the week before his 70th birthday, he shot a 69. In deference to his advancing years, it took him just a little more than two hours. According to Joe Dey, former Executive Director of the United States Golf Association, "The great Bobby Jones usually took not over three seconds from the moment of starting the address to the moment of impact."

In the 1996 U. S. Open at Oakland Hills, in Bloomfield Hills, Michigan, the pace of play was so slow in the last round that in many cases, there were 15 minute waits on tees before play could proceed. This can obviously play havoc with a player's tempo of play.

Given the amounts of money the pros are playing for and the variety of personalities involved, I can understand the recent advent of slower play, to some extent. However, in their newest rules the PGA, USGA, and LPGA provide greater penalties for slow play. I believe these organizations should be commended for their efforts in discouraging slow play.

The 1996 U. S. Open

At the 1996 U. S. Open Steve Jones, a relative unknown, beat the best golfers in the world on one of the toughest courses in the world, the Donald Ross designed Oakland Hills. His victory certainly tarnished the credibility of some supposedly knowledgeable golf pundits who predicted that one of the current stars would certainly win this event. Jones' victory was an excellent example of golf's unpredictability. Even more impressive, Jones had to qualify on a sectional basis and at that had to play off for a spot in the U. S. Open. The last time this happened was when Jerry Pate won the Open in 1976.

Here is what I think is an interesting insight in to the moral standards of the 1996 U. S. Open Champion. After his victory, Jones credited the newly published biography of Ben Hogan, entitled "Hogan", for providing him with inspiration to win the U. S. Open. The publisher of the book offered him $200,000 to endorse the book. Jones found portions of the book that contained profanities offensive, and for this reason, his condition for endorsement was for the publisher to remove the profanities from future printings of the book. The author refused to change his work and Jones turned down the publisher's endorsement offer.

Also in the 1996 Open, Davis Love's caddie was his brother Mark. Love finished second, three putting the 72nd green to miss tying Jones by one shot; a turn of events that I'm sure will stick in Love's mind for a great while to come. In fairness, Love was under tremendous pressure, and the championship speed of the greens at Oakland Hills were some of the toughest the pros had ever faced. The fairways were also undulating, making for very difficult shots from downhill and sidehill lies.

The rough was typically wrist-breaking, calling for great accuracy off the tees to narrow fairways to avoid it. Most pros hit a fade shot off the tee to keep the ball from rolling into the rough. All of these factors are typical of U. S. Open courses, and they remain perhaps the greatest test of golf skills anywhere. Needless to say, winning the U. S. Open takes great patience on the part of the golfer. It can be safely said that the toughest 18 holes in golf is the final 18 holes of the Open. We need to remember that golf is a game that will make a strong man cry.

A humorous note on the 1996 Open occurred when the suicide doctor Jack Kervorkian was spotted in the gallery. He was reported to have said to a reporter: "If Jack Nicklaus doesn't play well, I want you to tell him I'm here."

Caddies in Golf Today

Another trend which you could call negative in championship golf is the greater role the caddie is playing in tournament golf. I was in the gallery at the Solheim Cup Matches (the ladies' match equal to the Ryder Cup) in 1995 at the Greenbrier Championship Course in West Virginia where one player had her caddie stand directly behind her and remain there on a full shot to help the player make proper alignment. I really thought this was a violation of the rules but found out that at present it is not; only on the putting green must the caddie leave the position behind the ball when the player executes the shot. Golf was originally intended to be a game that the player alone performed; it was not intended to be a team effort.

This is not to take away from the key part played by the professional caddies in the success of their players. They do this job in a professional manner and within the rules of the game. Yet it strikes me that professional golf has to a great extent come to be more of a team effort than in the past. This is certainly not the intent of the game of golf. I liked it when the rule at the Masters was that the players had to use the caddies at Augusta National and couldn't bring their own caddies.

Today there is even a Tour Caddies Association which promotes the interests of caddies on the PGA Tour. Tour caddies presently make, on average, about $500 a week. A tournament winner usually pays the caddie 10% of the prize money. Some longtime tour caddies working for top players make over $100,000 a year.

Speaking of caddies, we owe the modern term caddy to Mary, Queen of Scots, who, as a young woman in the 17th century, was an avid golfer. Mary continued to play while at boarding school in France. As she made her way from tee to tee, she had students, who she called cadets, carry her clubs. Because the French pronunciation of cadet is "cah-day", it is believed that the word caddie is derived from the French pronunciation of the English term cadet.

Golfers in the past have relied on their sight and feel to judge distances. In the 1960's some golfers made their own yardage books. Around 1976 a yardage book was developed by a former tour caddie, George Lucas, who was also a very good golfer. His books are now very much accepted by the pros because of their accuracy and completeness. Lucas visits all of the PGA and LPGA tour courses at least every two years. He maps every detail of every hole, including sprinkler heads, bunkers, and other landmarks. His distance measurements are truly high-tech, and accurate to within inches. He compiles an accurate and concise book that is depended upon by many of the pros along with the advice of their caddies.

Weather conditions, humidity, prevailing winds,

condition of the course, and not to mention, how the golfer is feeling physically, are all variables that still call for human judgement in the choice of the club and how the shot should be hit. Chart books, improved equipment, and professional caddies all play a tangible and important part in lowering scores today. Golfers in the past did not have the advantage of such developments.

Golf on Television

Needless to say, one of the great changes to affect golf is the advent of television. In my opinion, regular television coverage of golf tournaments has done more to popularize golf than any other factor. A healthy economy surely has helped, too. Some people have attributed the popularity of golf to individual stars in the game. Some members of Arnie's army think that Palmer invented the game of golf. Yet no one can deny that his colorful and charismatic personality appealed to the public and contributed greatly to the increased popularity of the game. No doubt Palmer has done much for the game and has been an inspiration to many young professionals.

One of the negative aspects of television golf is that there are some poor commentators who talk too much and describe at length results of shots that are obvious to the viewer. Some of them repeat the amount of the prize money to the extent that it appears they are obsessed by it. Why some television producers feel the need to have commentators with stilted English accents is beyond me; their hyperbole at times is irritating. As a viewer, I think some commentators spend too much of the time focused on the action around the putting green, and even then, I find they seldom tell you the length or type of the putt the golfer is facing. The exception to all of this is that, in major national and international events, they do a superb overall job of picturing the play for those of us sitting at home. The camera work is just marvelous, with close-ups so good that you can read the brand name on the ball. Television networks are even using blimps and high towers to catch more of the action.

There are a number of articulate and high caliber commentators such as Johnny Miller, Ken Venturi, and Dave Marr, among others, that make watching golf on television truly interesting. Being previous winners of major championships, they are incredibly knowledgeable concerning the golf swing and tournament play and can provide the viewer with thought-provoking and educational analysis.

As a teenager, I was able to witness only one major golf event in the 1930's. Now, by simply turning on your television, you can view close up all of the major golf tournaments throughout the world. Further, and needless to say, you can view more of the action than if you were present. One of the disadvantages of television viewing is that you can't get a three-dimensional view so it is virtually impossible to appreciate the difficulty the player faces on severely undulating greens.

I was in the gallery at the Masters in 1960 when Arnold Palmer needed to birdie either the 17th or 18th hole in the last round to tie Ken Venturi who was already in the club house. It wouldn't have been wrong for Venturi to have visions of putting on that Green Jacket. Palmer proceeded to birdie not only the 17th hole but the 18th as well and won the tournament by one stroke. After watching Palmer sink a good size putt on the 17th green, I had to run to the 18th green to see the action. There had to be at least 30,000 people in that gallery. It was an exciting and thrilling experience to say the least; yet not an ideal way to view a golf tournament.

In later years I went to the Masters, and still do, to watch the practice rounds only. I then sit back in my home to view the action Thursday through Sunday and get to see a lot more on television. Forty years ago, 1956, the first Masters was televised. Since then, the popularity of golf has exploded, and so have the galleries. Televising this tournament in particular, which incidentally has the largest viewing audience of any other tournament, has undoubtedly contributed greatly to the popularity of golf. These major events are also extremely well covered, giving not only great coverage of all the action, but the commentary is usually well done. Wouldn't it be great if, for example, we had on video tape the action the year Bobby Jones made his grand slam in 1930.

One of the aspects of present day golf is the plethora of television commercials during golf events touting exaggerated claims of what some products will do for your golf game. It amuses me to see the television commercials advertising products with big name pros, inferring that if only you will use such and such balls, newly designed golf clubs, and special shoes that provide a launching platform to the booming drives you'll be able to hit, your golf game will rise to new levels. There are times when I almost feel compelled to immediately get up out of my chair in order to immediately run down to the golf shop and make a purchase. The fact of the matter is that most of the endorsing professionals have their clubs customized to their specific needs by the company they represent.

Any PGA Tour event has many equipment manufacturers represented, complete with a plethora of clubs to try and facilities to custom-build anything the pros want - all free of charge, of course.

Such is the way of a free capitalistic society. I

would say, though, that in the thirties you weren't faced with such tempting television commercials. As a matter of fact, you were just glad to have any old clubs or balls you could get. An interesting bit of history for those who are inclined to change putters frequently: the great Walter Hagen used the same putter throughout his entire career.

In the opinions of many, golf today is guilty of having become over-commercialized, and I believe there is some merit in that position. Obviously, though, professional golf does not have a monopoly on over-commercialization, for in other sports, it's far more prevalent. Yet, I think it's an unattractive reflection of our capitalistic society and needs to be tempered, but I, for one, am for capitalism, despite its drawbacks.

Tournament Galleries

There are some real changes in being a member of the gallery of golf tournaments now as compared to then. First off, and most obviously, galleries are much larger now, making it more difficult to view the action. In the past, there were no gallery ropes as there are now lining the fairways to restrain the gallery. An illustration of this occurred in the 1946 Masters won by the professional, Herman Keiser, who was paired with Sam Snead in the third round. Keiser was a short hitter and Snead was the longest hitter on the tour. He out drove Keiser by 50 yards or more at times. Spectators, unrestricted by gallery ropes, would gallop after Snead's ball, forcing Keiser to play many of his approach shots over their heads. In contrast, modern tournament golf calls for roped fairways, electronic leader boards, and fruit and water for the players on every tee.

The popularity of some tournaments, particularly the Masters, has caused a limit to be placed on the number of tickets sold to viewers of that tournament and, even at that, it is still difficult to view the action unless you're in the first row or two surrounding the tee or green. The PGA has developed what are called Stadium courses specifically designed to especially enable the gallery to view the action more easily. Despite all of this, some people have given up trying to view tournaments in person, opting instead to watch tournaments on television.

The behavior of galleries has remained pretty much the same since the 1930's. They cheer when a difficult putt is holed and groan when a putt rims the cup and stays out. For the most part, golf galleries' enthusiasm for the game remains unbounded.

As in the past, devoted spectators still come out in some of the most horrendous weather - rain and windy cold - to follow their favorite golfers, sometimes secretly hoping to emulate their swing by watching closely. This is often with the hope that the experience will improve the watcher's game. Overall, members of galleries at most golf tournaments are more knowledgeable about golf and golfers now than in the past. Some in the gallery can even spot and identify golfers just by their swings.

Demeanor and Dress on the Golf Course

Golfers, pros and amateurs alike, still talk to their ball when it's in flight, trying to persuade it to go where they want it to go, expressing their feelings with body language. Human nature being what it is, I expect this habit will never change, of which I am glad since it makes the game all the more colorful.

Golfers in the past were attired differently than those of today - a shirt and tie was common. The galleries followed suit and were usually quite well dressed, at least by today's standards. I can remember in the fifties being in the gallery at the Masters, seeing the women with an almost Easter parade appearance in their dress. The galleries and golfers now are attired in some eye-catching outfits, to say the least. It's striking that some of the affluent caddies are often better dressed than the players. This, of course, has changed not just in golf but in all areas of our life.

Some professionals now appear to be walking billboards, which I think is unattractive and detracts from the tradition of the game. Another trend in modern tournament play is that a few pros are wearing wraparound sunglasses, looking very much like secret service agents. I sort of expect the President of the United States to appear at any moment. In all seriousness, pros that wear sunglasses say that they simply help them to see better. Also, those that wear contact lenses while playing find that sunglasses keep their lenses from getting dry or dusty.

I understand, too, that showboating on the part of the professional golfer is important to some golf fans, for they are looking for entertainment. I'd like to distinguish showboating from a colorful personality. A golfer with a colorful personality adds to the attractiveness of watching golf. Showboating, in my opinion, is when the golfer deliberately and in a planned way invites attention. Snead, for example, who was certainly no Mister Personality in my opinion and had nothing contrived in his manner, was colorful because of his background and natural manner. I think there's lots of drama in championship golf regardless of the personalities involved.

Golf and Equal Opportunity

As a positive, the USGA, PGA, and LPGA have played a big role in providing opportunities for all to play championship golf, regardless of race or social standing. An interesting story related by Joe Dey, the first PGA tour commissioner, took place in the second U.S. Open Championship in 1896. There was a 16 year-old black caddie who wanted to play in the tournament. Several British professionals there said they wouldn't play if the boy was allowed to play. The president of the USGA said the caddie was going to play whether they played or not. He played, and so did they. That was a fellow named John Shippen, and he played successfully in the U.S. Open for 20 years thereafter.

An interesting bit of history regarding the problem of racial discrimination in golf involves the history of the PGA itself. The PGA was born in 1916 and one of the requirements was that members must be of the Caucasian race. It took nearly a half a century before that exclusion was removed from the rules in 1961. Charlie Sifford was the first Black to win a tournament with a mix of races as competitors.

An interesting development on the subject of race in golf is the story of Tiger Woods. He turned professional after winning his third consecutive National Amateur Championship in August of 1996. There really was nothing else left for him to win in amateur golf. As of this writing Tiger Woods has entered only eight professional events during his first three months as a pro, and has won two of them. He finished the year 1996 in 24th place on the money list with almost $800,000 in prize money. Pretty remarkable for a 20 year old rookie.

There is no question that Woods' entry into the professional ranks has been like a bomb shell landing on the tournament golf scene. He has elevated the game and stimulated enormous new interest as well as drawn bigger galleries. Considering the tremendous pressure of being in the spotlight he has handles himself very well.

His entry into professional golf has surely gotten the attention of the other Tour players, particularly the top ones. Some observers of the today's professional golf scene have speculated that there never could be another Nicklaus that could rise above and dominate so deep in great talent. Could they be wrong? Could Nicklaus be right when he says there may be 10 green jackets in Woods' future? Tom Lehman, chosen the best PGA Tour player for 1996 said, "Tiger Woods has made an incredible impact on the Tour. He's good for the Tour and gives us all a new challenge."

Tiger Woods has been named the 1996 Sports Illustrated Sportsman of the Year for symbolizing in character and performance the ideals of sportsmanship. This honor landed him on the cover of the December 23, 1996 issue of the magazine.

Woods has reportedly signed the largest single financial endorsement contract in the history of professional tournament golf - 60 million dollars over the next 5 years. Obviously without financial worries, Woods can now concentrate on trying to compile a great record as a professional. No one knows if he will really meet his full potential, as golf can be a very fickle game indeed. One thing for sure though, his high profile presence in the world of golf will greatly influence other minority athletes to turn more to the sport of golf.

Most recently, Tiger Woods won the 1997 Masters with a record breaking score of 18 under par. This was a truly phenomenal performance at a level that marks a new standard of play in the world of tournament golf.

Today, if a man or woman is good enough to play, regardless of his or her race, creed, or color, he or she can play. Organized golf can be especially proud of its record in this area. One of the other recent beneficial changes in golf is the opportunity for handicapped players to play the game. Millions now play with the support of the USGA. In Colorado, a golf course has been specially designed to allow access by golfers who are handicapped.

Another very positive aspect in golf today is the tremendous development of public golf courses in recent years, and the effect this has had in the increased popularity of golf. Today there are more public courses than there are private courses. However, golf is still out of financial reach for many, especially the young. Hopefully, with more public golf courses and possibly more par three courses the price of playing golf will come down so that more will be able to play the game.

Golf is no longer just a spectator sport. Presently there are about 24 million golfers in the United States. It's the amateurs who have provided the foundation of the game. Perhaps less than one percent of golfers can play the kind of golf that even approaches the caliber of golf of the tour professionals or top amateurs. We've got to be careful not to take the game away from the amateur and not to let it revolve around the tour professional. As was said by Jack Burke, Jr., former Masters champion, "Golf is more than just a game; we need to preserve the challenge and spirit of the game."

Qualifying to be a Professional
on the PGA Tour Now and in the Past

In the beginning of professional tour golf there were few tour events. In 1929 the winter tour consisted of only 8 tournaments. Until recent years professionals qualified to play in tournaments by playing a qualifying round on Mondays before the tournament. Pros competed to fill the number of places that were available.

To qualify for tournaments now, players must be qualified to play on the Tour, unless they have a sponsor exemption. To qualify for the PGA Tour they must first pay an entry fee of $3,000 plus expenses. Of course, to be competitive, they must be pretty much a scratch handicap player, and they have to have their club professional recommend them. They play in a series of regional qualifying events, and the 188 who survive go on to a final event where they play 18 holes for six consecutive days. In 1996 there were 1100 pros playing for the 40 spots available on the 1997 Tour. A similar qualifying program is followed for the LPGA Tour.

The PGA Tour qualifying tournament is not just for the young, up-and-coming professional hopefuls. In 1996 20 of the players had at least one PGA Tour victory in the past, but did not finish in the top 125 players in earnings which would have automatically qualified them. Twenty one of the contestants had one more than one million dollars in official PGA Tour earnings. Players the caliber of Bob Estes and Bobby Wadkins were not among the top 40 qualifiers.

To say that Q-School competiton is gruelling is an understatement. The hopeful pros literally dread the event. As has been said, the Q-School is the most depressing event in sports. To survive and qualify, one has to have not only great golf skills but really be on his game mentally in order to survive the mind-boggling pressure of that week.

The total number of players seeking their fortune on the PGA Tour today reflects the tremendous depth of competiton that exists today which did not exist in the past.

Senior Golf

One of the positive developments of golf now as compared to then is the development of the Senior Tour. In the past, there was hardly much of a regular tour, much less a Senior Tour. Despite the doubts at the time of it's possible success, the Senior Tour has proven to be enormously successful and popular. In this year, 1996, the senior professionals will play a full schedule of 40-some tournaments. In deference to age, I suppose, they play three rounds instead of the four played in regular tour events. Bob Goalby, a former Masters champion, was one of the prime movers in getting the Senior Tour off the ground.

The opportunity to continue play for the professional golfer over age 50 is tremendous. The prize money for these players on this tour has accelerated at an amazing rate. Many of the top senior players are earning as much or more now than they did when they played the regular tour. Some of the top winners in 1995 were in the million dollar category. For the older golf fans, this has been great in that they can identify easily with many of the stars from the past and enjoy their really outstanding caliber of play.

It was interesting to me, in the recent Legends of Golf Classics, to see that there was an additional grouping for those players over the age of 60. One of golf's greatest champions who is now age 85, Sam Snead, played and played well. This is a great inspiration for us senior amateurs.

In the past, when a championship golfer reached his forties, he was out of the picture as far as tournament golf was concerned. Now golfers in their forties are winning major events and looking forward to playing on the Senior and Super Senior Tours.

The fine professional golfer, Julius Boros (whose son Guy is now a successful player on the regular tour) won the PGA Championship in 1968 at the age of 48, the oldest golfer to ever do so. In 1986 Jack Nicklaus won the Masters at the age of 46. Tom Kite won the U. S. Open in 1992 while in his early forties. All of these wins were remarkable performances by men who years ago would have been considered old men in the world of golf and completely out of it.

The longevity of professional golfers is a great change and surely has increased the popularity of the sport. I expect that the improved health and the interest the pros have in staying in the best possible physical condition has a bearing on all of this. Yet I also think that the impact of television, the tremendous commercialization of golf, and a strong economy have all played a part as well.

Unfortunately, there is no question that when we age, vision is diminished with the accompanying loss of the ability to judge distances and depth. This is not to leave out creaking knees, bad backs, and the loss of muscular flexibility and strength. Eventually, like it or not, if we live long enough we fall apart in one way or another. Before I leave this subject there is a story of two players. The one with poor eye sight and the other with a failing memory. After one teed off, he asked his companion, "Did you see where it went?" The other said, "Yes I did, but I can't remember where."

Match Play vs. Medal Play

In the past, one of the four major golf events, the PGA
Championship, was played as match play. An interesting
bit of golf history is the outstanding performance of Walter
Hagen in match play tournaments. He won the PGA five
times and four times in succession. He was the master of
match play golf, not to mention that he won two U. S. Opens
and four British Opens in medal play. One of his many
psychological tricks in match play was to concede short
putts to his opponent early on and then make him putt out
all putts later in the match when the pressure was on.

As you perhaps know, in match play score is kept
by the winning of holes rather than by total number of
strokes. The hole is won by the player who holes the ball
in the fewest strokes. The reckoning of holes is kept by
terms such as so many "holes up" or "all square" and so
many holes to play. Amateur tournaments of 18 or 36 holes
are usually held with this format. In stroke play, sometimes
called medal play, the competitor who plays the stipulated
rounds or round in the fewest strokes is the winner. This is
the most popular format for professional golfers. Which
format better tests the skills of the golfer is debatable. In
match play the player tends to gamble more. For example,
firing at the flagstick that's in a difficult position in order to
win the hole. If they should make a high score and lose
that hole, they can put that score behind them and go on to
the next hole. In medal or stroke play, the player tends to
be more conservative, knowing that the total score for the
18 or 36 holes is what is all important.

The National Amateur reverted from match play to
medal play in 1965. This change was generally not well
received, and in 1973 the USGA changed the format to 36

holes of medal play with the low 64 players playing the rest of the tournament in match play. I think this was a good compromise and retained the benefits of both styles of play.

All of the regular tour events are held with a medal play format. There are still some team match play tournaments played late in the year which are not counted as regular tour events. I hardly think the tour events will ever revert to match play. The tremendous influence of television on golf and its commercial impact makes match play unattractive. It's held that audiences would diminish greatly if the favored stars were eliminated early on and two little known players should end up alone in the final matches. All of this, of course, is debatable. It's interesting to note that, in the USGA's contract with the television networks, they have an agreement that the network televise the finals of the match play of the National Amateur which is usually held in the fall of the year. I think the USGA is to be commended for encouraging the survival of this very exciting form of competitive golf.

An interesting tournament that is played as stroke play yet took on the aspect of match play was the final day of play in the Masters in April, 1996. Greg Norman and Nick Faldo were paired together as the last group to play and were the only real contenders during the final 18 holes. In effect, they were playing head to head golf that had all the flavor of match play and was very exciting to watch. Faldo won with a brilliant 67 after starting out the final 18 holes seven shots behind Norman, ending up five shots ahead. Great television viewing, I think.

It's interesting that in the Ryder Cup matches, in which the best professionals in the United States play the best in Great Britain and in Europe, part of the format is match play. The Walker Cup matches, where the best amateurs of the United States play the best in Britain, also have a format that includes match play. This can make for very exciting golf. When the Ryder Cup matches were changed to include the European players on the British team, there is no question they became much more competitive, and the event's popularity has improved tremendously. It has become one of the major sporting events of the year with a vast television audience.

As you perhaps know, for many years this event has been rather one-sided in favor of the United States. In 1995 the British and European team won the matches, making the event even more interesting. Their winning again points up the growing strength of the international players in the world of golf. The event will be played for the first time in Spain in 1997.

The Human Side

A factor often overlooked in the success of a champion golfer is the strength gained from a good relationship between a player and his wife and family. A wife in the gallery rooting for her husband has one of the toughest roles to play in golf, living through all of the ups and downs of her husband's play. Ben Hogan, I'm sure, would have agreed that his wife, Valerie, was all important to his success. They had a good, solid marriage. It's interesting that now and then a tour pro has enlisted his wife as his caddie. Steve Stricker, while playing as a member of the United States Team in the President's Cup, had his wife caddying for him. There is no denying that this reflects a wonderful relationship on their part - saves money, too. On the other hand, no one can deny that being separated from family presents a special set of problems for the tour golf pro. These issues are surely not easy to contend with.

Because of the need for intense concentration

playing on courses that are extreme challenges to their golf skills, the tour player can be emotionally drained after finishing a tournament. This is especially true in the play of major events. This sort of experience makes it difficult for players to stay "up" in tournament after tournament. Some players have the temperament to better cope with this factor than others. In the past you would think that since there were so many fewer tournaments that this would not be a problem. Yet, it is interesting that Bobby Jones retired after his grand slam at the age of 28. Also, Byron Nelson retired form tournament golf at the age of 34 shortly after winning his amazing eleven straight tournaments in 1945. That year, he won a total of 18 tournaments with a stroke average of 68.33, a full stroke better than any Vardon Trophy winner ever. Many tour pros are just getting started in their late 20's or early 30's in today's golf world.

Bobby Locke once made some comments that are quite relevant to the mental side of golf. Locke was a great international player, a multiple time winner of the British Open, successful invader of the U. S. Tour and, in his time, widely considered the foremost wizard on the green. He cleverly stated that the most difficult aspect of the game was to stay physically and mentally relaxed throughout a round of tournament golf. It's interesting that he attributed this ability to his success. He said that it's not easy to maintain such an attitude, but that doing so was all important. He went on to say that mental and physical tension was the greatest cause of the downfall of the tournament golfer.

As an aside, an unusual story involving Bobby Locke took place at St. Andrews, Scotland, in 1957 on the way to winning his fourth British Open. He was on the last hole on the final day and hit his shot to the home green four feet from the hole. His fellow competitor, Bruce

Crampton, asked Locke to mark his ball away from Crampton's line by a putter head length. When Locke made his putt, he failed to return the ball to its original position. He didn't realize this until later in the day when it was brought to the attention of the officials. News reel film confirmed the rule violation. However, the British Open Claret Jug had already been presented and the tournament had come to a close. The rules officials met and discussed the situation at length. Common sense prevailed, and they decided to take no action and Locke retained the trophy. Locke had won the tournament by three shots. Thus, even if he had been charged with the two stroke penalty for the rules infraction he would have still won by one stroke.

A modern term now used to describe the professional who is playing well is that he's "in the zone." That, of course, describes a player who is completely focused on his play and concentrating at a very high level. There was no such a term in the past, but I expect it's the same mental state Johnny Goodman felt when he shot his record second round 66 in winning the U. S. Open in 1933.

Money Present and Past

The amounts of the prize money now as compared to then is fantastic. When Ralph Guldahl finished second to amateur Johnny Goodman in the 1933 U. S. Open, he received the top prize money of one thousand dollars. In a recent tournament played in March of 1996 at the Doral in Florida, the winner, Greg Norman, received three hundred and twenty four thousand dollars. Even considering the value of the dollar in 1933 as compared to the present, that's a staggering increase in prize money. Greg Norman became the leading all-time money winner

in 1996 by passing the ten million dollar mark. The winner
of the Players Championship this year, 1996, was Fred
Couples. He received a first prize of six hundred thirty
thousand dollars. This reflects a dramatic change of the
financial reward found in professional golf.

Today's professionals who are affluent enough
have a staff of advisers that includes agents, lawyers, and
accountants to take care of money management matters.
This was hardly a problem for the struggling golf
professionals in the past. Another development is the use
by some professionals of sports psychologists, gurus, and
assorted golf instructors. No doubt, all of this is necessary
now that professional golf has become so sophisticated.
It's interesting to note that many professionals turn to
fellow players for help and guidance, and this speaks well
for their profession especially when the veteran is
supportive of the newcomer.

An interesting story written by Jimmy Demaret,
the great Masters champion of years gone by, relating to
his experience as a tour player in Florida during those
lean years, is that during a practice round, the players
would deliberately hit their balls into an orange grove,
load up their bags with fruit, and be on their way. This
was a supplement to their meager diets.

Sportsmanship in Golf

An impressive display of sportsmanship and
comradeship took place in the final round of the
Masters in April 1996. Nick Faldo and Greg Norman
were paired together as the last twosome and as leaders
in the final round. At the start of the round Norman had a
six-shot lead over Faldo. For the newspaper pundits it
was a forgone conclusion that Norman would be winning

his first Masters green jacket. It was not to be. Faldo shot the best round of the day, a 67, and Norman shot a 78. Faldo won by five shots. At Augusta I don't think a round of 78 is unusual even for the best of them, and a 67 is certainly extraordinary. In my view the results certainly were because of Norman's six over par round, but also because Faldo kept the heat on him throughout the round with his great round of 67. Norman would have had to shot a par 72 to beat him - no small feat in any event and surely not easy in the last round of the Masters. My point here is that I don't think Faldo got the credit he deserves, while Norman was faulted for what was described as a collapse.

At any rate, on the 18th green, after Faldo sunk his putt for a birdie and the win, he immediately went over to Norman and hugged him with great emotion - a wonderful example of sympathy, sportsmanship, and again camaraderie. I've never seen anything quite like it before.

Jack Nicklaus, among many others, set a fine example of good sportsmanship. He's not only a great winner, but a great loser as well. After losing he can look his opponent in the eye, smile and say "Well done."

The civility and honorable standards of sportsmanship and gentlemanly conduct set by the game as compared to many other sports is on a high level, and always has been. It is all important that golf etiquette, obeying rules, and high standards of honesty on the part of the players continue, despite the diminishing of these characteristics today in some aspects of our culture and society.

One of the examples, and there are many, that make this point is taken from a recent article in *Links* golf magazine about a modern golf professional, Tom Lehman. In the 1990 qualifying school for the PGA Tour, Tom Lehman called a penalty on himself when a stiff breeze caused his ball to move slightly after he addressed it. He wound up missing the cut by one stroke. Lehman explained: "If a breach of the rules had occurred, and I didn't call it on myself, I couldn't look at myself in the mirror. You're only as good as your word. And your word wouldn't be worth much if you can't even be honest with yourself."

Lehman's loss at the Q-school sent him to the Ben Hogan Tour (now the Nike Tour) in 1991 where he set a Hogan Tour record. The confidence he gained on the Hogan Tour has led to Lehman's two PGA Tour victories and a second place finish in the 1996 U. S. Open. He most recently won the 1996 British Open played at Royal Lytham and St. Annes Golf Club in England with 13 under par, two strokes better than Ernie Els and Mark McCumber and three in front of Nick Faldo. Tom Lehman is now considered to be among the world's best golfers.

The code of honor of the tour players is the highest possible. Golf's high ethical standards are setting an important example in this area for all, and especially for young people.

Tournament Golf Past and Present

A great difference between tournament golf today as compared to the past is the number of tournaments played by professional golfers. Bobby Jones, one of golf's truly great players of all time, during the period 1923 to 1930, entered a total of 28 tournaments, an average of 3.6 tournaments a year. The average pro of that era held down a club job to help support himself, as there were fewer tournaments to play in, not to mention the meager prize money awarded. Now the average tour pro plays about 25 to 30 tournaments per year, and top amateurs not far from it. Obviously, this gives the pros of today a greater opportunity to hone and sharpen their skills. However, the down side to playing in so many tournaments is they face a very difficult task in trying to stay "up" mentally in tournament after tournament.

Another change that I see in tournament golf today is that the greens sometimes are softer as a result of modern watering systems and the way they're constructed. It often permits the pros, with their great accuracy, to hit for the flagsticks and get lower scores.

Because of the great condition of the greens and the architecture of the greens themselves on the regular tour, the players tend to play target golf - firing shots as close to the flagstick as they can. This type of play is in marked contrast to the creative shot-making required by courses on which the major events are played, and particularly the types of courses played in Great Britain.

An often overlooked group that does great work in tournament play, as well as everyday play, are the golf course superintendents and their staffs. This is true particularly in the face of bad weather where courses have to be maintained for play despite heavy rainfall. They are pretty much the unsung heroes of golf.

Another note of progress for golf and all the tours is the tremendous role their tournaments play in raising large sums of money for worthwhile charities throughout the country year after year. To date, the PGA Tour has raised over three hundred million dollars for charities. In the past, there was not enough money around to contribute to charities.

The Major Tournaments

The four major events in golf are now, as you perhaps know, the Masters, the U. S. Open, the PGA, and the British Open. I've had the pleasure to see them all firsthand numerous times. These events, in my opinion, are held on courses that are classics, and that really, really test the skills of the golfers. There are many challenges facing golfers playing a championship type course. One is the severely undulating greens that are mega quick and are as hard as marble, making putting a real challenge. At the 1996 Masters, one pro joked he marked his ball on the green with a dime and the dime slid off the green. He had to use a quarter instead. Also, they are faced with undulating fairways in the landing areas of their drives. These fairways present a difficult second shot from downhill or side hill lies to greens that require accurately and well hit second shots.

However, there is more to these golf courses than meets the eye. I remember in the year of the U.S. Open at The Country Club in Brookline, the course which I caddied on as youngster, when Palmer lost to Julius Boros in the play-off. Palmer stated that it was a course where he had to use every club in his bag. On the subject of the difficult test of golf skills at the U. S. Open Tournament, Frank Tatum, former president of the USGA, said "We're not trying to humiliate the greatest players in the world. We are trying to identify them."

The high level of skill required to win in the major events, I think, is clearly evident when you see the winning score at about par for the 72 holes in the U. S. Open. Yet in many regular tour events you see players as much as 20 or more under par. The tests of shot making on some regular tour courses as compared to courses for major events are simply not up to the same standards.

As an amateur, I'd like to share an experience with you that you may find interesting. It's not relevant to the state of golf, now and then, except that it involves the great Pebble Beach Course in California where Goodman defeated Jones in the National Amateur in 1929. This course, with very few changes, is pretty much the same now, as it was in 1929.

I took a week's vacation to work for the television network doing the 1982 broadcast of the U. S. Open at Pebble Beach. My brother, Theodore, and sister, Evelyn, live nearby the course. I was assigned to the 15th green and was there throughout the tournament. My job was to relay information to the director, name the players who were approaching the green, the action of play into the green and on the green, etc.. The 15th hole at Pebble Beach is a slightly downhill, straight away, par four, 397 yard hole to a fairly undulating green, surrounded by deep rough, except for the fairway entrance to the green. From the tee, the left side is protected by large pines. To the right is out of bounds - the famous 17 mile drive. The way you line up off the tee welcomes you to hit right, but you want to try to get the ball on the left side of the fairway without aiming left into the trees. This puts the player in the best position for the second shot into the green.

After four full days of watching play there, I naturally had a pretty good idea as to the best way the pros should play the hole, even though I couldn't do it myself. First of all, let me say that Pebble Beach is set up very differently for the Open than when they play the Crosby there every year (now known as the AT&T Pebble Beach National Pro-Am). For the Open, the fairways are narrower, the rough deeper, and the greens cut more closely and hence are faster. The flagstick placements were so that, if a player was sucked into playing for the flagstick and didn't hit the shot exactly right, he could be in big trouble. On some greens, if the ball was not hit far enough, it would spin back off the green down a slope. If the ball landed too far and above the flagstick, the golfer was faced with a difficult fast downhill putt that, unless he sank it, could end up four or five feet past the hole at best. I might say, too, that in June, the month the Open was played , it was exceptionally cool and windy with morning fog - so cool that I had to wear a wind breaker and warm clothes.

The drive on that hole had to be in the fairway or else the player would find a very difficult second shot, depending on how deep in the rough his ball was. The second shot had to be hit to the part of the green, depending on the flagstick placement, that would avoid threeputting. The second iron shot had to be hit flush with the right amount of spin to hold the green. One player hit his second shot into the rough, short and to the right of the green, and they had a tough time finding the ball. When he did hit his third shot, two balls came out. Fortunately, there was no penalty for that.

The players that managed to one putt, and they were few and far between, and two putt, had to hit their second shot to the part of the green that made that more possible. Obviously, this put a premium on accurate iron play into the green which is a characteristic requirement for U. S. Open type courses, For getting out of the wrist-breaking rough, I can understand the comment that the golfer has to be strong. Needless to say, accuracy off the tee to avoid all this, is the hallmark of any U.S. Open champion, which I think is as it should be.

After observing for four full days, I came to the conclusion that, when they say that the ability of the player to manage his play on the course is perhaps the biggest element in successful play, I believe it. The experience there brought home to me the importance of the ability of the player to accurately read putts, particularly on the lightning fast and undulating greens.

I felt really important, being inside the ropes in such a prestigious event, and it was to me a real education in what the pro has to face in the U. S. Open. No wonder some of them have a headache when they finish the round. Before anyone gains the wrong impression, I was a bit player on the television staff. They paid me the grand total of one hundred dollars for my work. I wouldn't do it again, but it was an education in tournament golf. Try as I might, I couldn't get in any of the camera views, and I was disappointed that my friends back on the east coast never got to see me.

But it was quite a thrill at the close to be able to walk down the fairway and be able to watch Tom Watson sink his pitch out of the rough into the hole on the par three 17th and thereby, eventually beat out Jack Nicklaus for the title that year.

In Conclusion

Golf, as we know it, has come a long way since its beginnings in Scotland 400 years ago when Scottish shepherds first swung at stones with their sheep crooks, from the St. Andrews Course, to Yonkers, New York, in 1888 by the Apple Tree Gang, to the present day. At the same time, looking at the state of our society and culture today as compared to 50 or 60 years ago, vast changes have taken place. Despite the general deterioration and decline of the ethics and morality of our culture, on balance looking at the long view and taking everything into consideration, I think the pluses outweigh the minuses. Having lived as a youngster through one of history's severest depressions and being invited by our government to participate in World War II in the South Pacific theater of war, I can say without hesitation that I'd rather be living now than then.

Yet, when I think of the difficult times the subject of this story, Johnny Goodman, lived through, my political bias shows through with some questions. If the intrusive federal government of today, with some of its cradle-to-grave helping programs existed then, would his story have been different? So far, the government has not intruded into golf, except in the area of taxes. What if there had been some sort of government program to assist Johnny Goodman with some sort of welfare support that would have made it unnecessary for him to scratch out a living when he was orphaned? He would never have had to caddie and work at other jobs to support himself and his younger brothers and sisters. He then may not have been driven and motivated by his circumstances of poverty to succeed as he did. This is pure speculation, but I do wonder. Would there have been a Johnny Goodman story to tell?

I would have to conclude that there are far more positive aspects than there are negative aspects to the development of golf in my observation over the last 60 years. Despite the negatives I think the sport is healthy and growing.

Will there ever be another amateur to win the U. S. Open as Johnny Goodman did in 1933? He would have to be of the likes of Jack Nicklaus, who nearly won as an amateur in the Open of 1960, finishing second to Arnold Palmer at Cherry Hills. Someone who started golf early, had excellent instructions to develop a sound swing, played in lots of tournaments like Nicklaus, and who won two National Amateurs at an early age. Someone smart enough to manage his game on tough golf courses. Someone who was young enough and brash enough not to be awed by a major tournament like the Open. Someone who had a cavalier disregard for the established stars. That player may come along one day, and I hope he does. It would be good for the game.

The history of championship golf is replete with human examples of what has made America great. The incredible story of Johnny Goodman is one of these great examples. Despite the disadvantage of being born into poverty, being an orphan, and overcoming barrier after barrier, he rose to the top of the world of golf. Only in America could a story like that be told.

*Additional copies of this book may be ordered
by remitting $28.00 to cover the cost
of the book including sales tax and postage
along with your address to:*

Curtis Publishing
P. O. Box 17693
Richmond, VA 23226

Please make checks payable to Walter J. Curtis